T0339796

RUNNING OUT

RUNNING OUT:

How Global Shortages
Change the Economic Paradigm

Pablo Rafael Gonzalez

Algora Publishing
New York

ISBN 0-87586-419-8 trade paper
ISBN 0-87586-420-1 hard cover
ISBN 0-87586-421-X ebook

Library of Congress Cataloging-in-Publication Data —

Gonzalez, Pablo Rafael.
    Running out: How Global Shortages Change the Economic Paradigm / Pablo
Rafael Gonzalez.
        p. cm.
    Includes bibliographical references.
        ISBN 0-87586-419-8 (trade paper: alk. paper) — ISBN 0-87586-420-1 (hard
cover: alk. paper) — ISBN 0-87586-421-X (ebook)   1.   Nonrenewable natural
resources. 2.   Natural resources. 3.   Energy consumption. 4.   Petroleum industry and
trade. 5.   Scarcity. I. Title.

    HC59.3.G66 2005
    333.8'2—dc22
                                    2005033248

Printed in the United States

To all the Children of the World

This work is an expression of optimistic rationalism, a reflection on the need to find a solution for the two most pressing problems confronting humanity in the 21st century: the scarcity and degradation of natural resources — caused by human neglect — and the antinomy represented by the need to use energy and to protect the environment.

Acknowledgements

Thanks to all the friends who have kindly helped me in this effort. My acknowledgment to Professor Domingo Felipe Maza Zavala, one of the most brilliant economists of Latin America, who for many years generously has attended my needs for advice, and to Algora Publishing for their assistance in preparing the English-language manuscript.

"The reader is pretty much asleep. The system is designed to keep him in that state. Therefore, the main objective of a literary work and of an essay must be to wake up that reader, to make him participate in the discussion and contribute to the solution, so he can reach his own conclusions based on the parameters and the information that he receives from his reading."

— Carlos Fuentes

(in the program "A Fondo" with Joaquín Soler Serrano, TVE Broadcasting, Spain.)

TABLE OF CONTENTS

INTRODUCTION

In the current century, perhaps in our lifetime, the world will face a shocking scarcity of natural resources as a consequence of overexploitation and pollution around the world. This represents a change of the economic paradigm but, more important, an unprecedented and mind-boggling challenge for humanity.

This book sets out to prove that we are on the path to the exhaustion of renewable and nonrenewable natural resources, especially water and conventional oil. The paradigm that predominates in the minds of economists is that capital that is the scarce factor of production; but the following chapters aim to show that, in the 21st century, natural resources must be the priority. Until now, production has not been the main worry of economists. Their main worry has been distribution of the results of production. Ever-growing production has been possible as man expanded his range across the globe and discovered more and more natural resources, and rapid population growth has meant there were generally enough hands to do the work; thus, it has mainly been capital that was seen as limited in supply. From now on, a different problem will loom ever larger. Achieving production goals will be more difficult for one simple reason: every day the supply of natural resources will be tighter. This represents a 180-degree shift in traditional economic ideas. This work analyzes the global scarcity of natural resources as a new paradigm for the economy.

The existence of production and reserves statistics for the last sixty years makes conventional oil the easiest resource to track, as well as one of the most essential to modern civilization; the following chapters will take oil as an example of the resources whose imminent exhaustion is being recklessly accelerated, and to demonstrate that the same trend can be seen with other important resources.

To a large extent the depletion of earth's resources is a consequence of man's actions; but if the overexploitation of nature and the increasing pollution continue, humanity will confront serious survival problems in a very short while.

The main premise is unquestionable: if even renewable natural resources are disappearing — as is proven by the increasing number of species in extinction, the deterioration of water sources and the disappearance of a good part of the world's forests — then clearly the overexploitation of *non*renewable natural resources must lead inexorably to their exhaustion. Each opinion or interpretation is backed up with statistical evidence. When I talk about the extinction of species, I present international statistics on birds, mammals and plants. When I assert that there is a downward trend worldwide for production or that we are on the way to using up our water sources or destroying the forests, I prove it with the corresponding official figures. When I say that oil supplies are being used up, it is because production and reserves trends indicate just that. The interpretations made in the following chapters are a result of the analysis of objective mathematical reality.

I began this research motivated by a desire to understand the forces that move oil prices from one extreme to another. I did not understand how a fundamental product like oil, which may be considered vital for humanity, could drop, for example, to $7 per barrel in the first months of 1999 and quadruple in price just a few months later. Why, in recessionary times, is oil production not significantly curtailed? Which forces move the prices toward the extremes? What is the logic they follow? What will happen in the future? What will the oil industry be doing in the years to come? Will petroleum products be replaced by other energy sources?

When I began to dig deeper, I understood that beyond the answers to those questions there is a hidden reality that is fundamental. It is one of the most important news items of the century but, paradoxically, this reality remains hidden, covered with a veil and jealously guarded. The truth is that the world's oil is quickly being depleted. The new reserves that have been discovered are not great enough to fill the void left by the exploitation of productive fields. As a consequence, I redirected my research to focus more intensely on oil reserves throughout the world. My first reaction was a logical deduction. Obviously, I said to myself, oil is a finite product and, consequently, it cannot go on forever. But how long will it last? According to my calculations, not long at all. And I asked myself what is the reason — if there is tangible, real evidence that the oil supply is dwindling — why this does not appear to occupy the government's attention, nor that of the oil companies nor the major world press? I checked first in my own country, which is one of the main oil-producing countries of the world, Venezuela. I consulted industry experts and academics, and they assured me there was nothing to worry about because there is plenty of oil in the world for many years to come.

But when I directed my research toward the United States, things looked different. I found that the topic is being studied seriously in certain academic circles since the thesis of geologist King M. Hubbert was upheld: he predicted that US oil production would begin to shrink in 1969, a prediction that came true the following year, 1970; and since then production has not recovered. I found works by university professors and experts from the oil companies themselves which confirmed that, indeed, oil is quickly disappearing from the world as a whole.

I asked myself if I should go ahead. This topic is very little discussed and is not properly appreciated by the public — not even in oil-producing countries — so I decided to continue. For if the hypothesis that oil supplies are on the verge of being exhausted is correct, as it seems to be, then we must do everything possible to make the world take notice. It is imperative that we become more conscious of the very finite character of oil; it is a very scarce good, indeed, a gift of nature that man may exhaust at his own peril.

And oil is part of a circle of resources that are closely linked to the preservation of life on this planet. Every day, without any sense of restraint, man destroys more and more of the forests — and that, in turn, affects our sources of water. This decreases the options for producing hydroelectric energy, among other things. The destruction of nature is a self-reinforcing cycle that forces us to consume more fuel and create more pollution; this process is a constant feedback loop. Furthermore, when I began to review the figures on natural resources, and world food production and distribution in the different continents, I saw that a similar phenomenon is happening with water and food, as well. Less water is available every day due to pollution, and world food production is growing slower than the population's rate of consumption. And another point struck me: huge areas of the world still lack electricity and other luxuries that the rest of us take for granted. How will they get their fair share, if the energy/pollution situation is already at a crisis point?

They say "there's nothing new under the sun," but in that moment I understood that the world is indeed facing a new phenomenon — the global scarcity of natural resources — and that this represents a complete change in the economic paradigm that has been in place until now. This new reality calls for a change in economic theories that have focused on the factors of production. Resources, not capital, are now the most limited factor of production.

And while I was pulling together my research, an event occurred that will surely change world relationships for a long time: the attack on the World Trade Center in New York City, September 11, 2001. This event will have a special impact on relations with the countries of the Middle East and on the oil situation across the globe. From September to December 2001, oil prices dropped by half. The price of crude was around $30 in September and $15 in December. The attack impelled the United States economy further into the recession that had begun in the first trimester of 2001. But even so, oil production did not decrease significantly; nor did it do so even in the Great Depression of the 1920s. In 1929-1930, it went down only by five percent. How can that be?

Experience shows that recessions are temporary and that oil production will continue growing. But reality also warns that oil prices may now be heading upwards for the long term. In 2005 oil already hit a level that was unthinkable before, and this while the public still has no idea how scarce and precious a commodity it is.

Every day there is less oil — that's the geological reality. More than two thirds of the world's oil reserves are in the Middle East — that's the geopolitical reality.

But in the end, after a long period of research, the strongest impression that remained with me was that the crisis of a permanent oil shortage was equaled by the crisis caused by the pollution that petroleum use generates. We need the energy derived from fossil fuels; no adequate substitution for them has been discovered. But if we continue using energy the way we do, the damage that is caused to the entire eco-system is of such magnitude that in a very short time there will be no life left on Earth. What can we do?

GENERAL SYNTHESIS

The first chapter asserts that economic doctrine has not yet considered the scarcity of natural resources caused by over-exploitation and pollution as an economics problem. Recognizing the global scarcity of natural resources and specifically of water and oil represents a new vision, a new focus on the factors of production.

In the second chapter, the fundamental dilemma of the book is presented in terms of the question whether we have enough natural resources to guarantee the feeding and employment of the world population, regardless of how that population may grow. Income distribution among the nations, rates of oil consumption and the changes that may occur in the near future are all considered. The unsustainable course of development based on the overexploitation of natural resources and the debt burden of the developing countries are pondered as well. It presents the remarkable changes in the global population's structure in recent decades, especially the one known as Demographic Transition — the increase of longevity indexes and decrease in birth rates indexes — that has been accentuated in the developed nations.

The new economic paradigm must address the distribution of earth's scarce resources, and conclude in a modern equation that looks to achieve economic growth and employment while consuming the least possible resources and generating the least possible pollution.

In the third chapter, the correlation between population growth and all the other variables is analyzed.

Chapter 4 explains the effects that would predictably derive from the shortage of resources. Thus far we have had only a foretaste of what may be coming, because the oil crises of 1973 and 1979 were understood to be artificial. That is, they were caused by a change in policy on the part of the Arab oil countries, not because no more oil could be found. The two main options facing the world today are presented: to preserve oil consumption rationally or to continue expending it without limitation. Afterward, some consideration is given to the environmental effects of oil exploitation.

The hypothesis that oil is running out is documented by official statistics on oil production and oil reserves. Reserves are declining measurably in various parts of the world, in a way that has no parallel in history. In the past, mankind chose to replace wood and coal with other fuels because they were more efficient or more convenient, not because the old fuel was running out all over the world.

The price of oil has never reflected its true scarcity. In only six years, between 1974 and 1980, it leapt by 3,200% from $1.25 per barrel to $40 per barrel. In 2005, it jumped dramatically again. We can anticipate even worse shocks in the near future when it becomes clear to everyone that the oil supply is being depleted very quickly.

It is apparent that some of the world leaders are aware of the oil shortage, and that they do not admit it in public for political and economic reasons; of course, if they admitted it, the chaos would be uncontrollable.

That oil depletion is real cannot seriously be questioned. Even many "renewable" natural resources that should not have disappeared have, nevertheless, done just that. If even renewable resources are being used up, how much more readily will the non-renewable resources disappear? The extinction of animal and plant species and deforestation indexes all point in the same direction. As well, shrinking lakes and the decrease of river flows and greater pollution have caused serious problems for the supply of drinking water, irrigation, and for hydroelectricity generation in many regions. Two of the biggest countries in Latin America, Brazil and Venezuela, had to institute severe water rationing in 2001. Lake Chad in Africa has shrunk by 90% and "we face increasing tensions and instability as rising populations compete for life's most precious of precious resources," according to UNEP chief Klaus Toepfer.[1] These facts are considered signs of what could happen in other regions of the world.

Subsequently, a correlation is made among population, food production worldwide, water and energy, to demonstrate — with official figures — the observable deterioration in the supply of these indispensable commodities. This is correlated with the effects of pollution. Historical examples such as the Potosí Mines — the greatest silver reserve in the world since the 16th century — are evidence of the exhaustion of natural resources. And the problem of growth limits is presented once again, to reach the conclusion that humanity faces a massive deterioration of natural resources.

In Chapter 6 the oil production figures for 2000 are presented. Chapter 7 explores the predicted global demand for oil to 2020, on the basis of a study by the United States Department of Energy. Chapter 8 provides and interprets sta-

---

1. "Africa Lakes under Strain as Populations Rise," November 01, 2005. Wangui Kanina, Reuters. Online at http://www.enn.com/water.html?id=283.

tistics on the world's oil production, reserves and consumption from the 1940s to the 2000s, demonstrating that oil production has grown at a significantly higher rate than the discover of reserves, a fact that in itself proves that oil is being exhausted on a worldwide scale. A similar situation exists with regard to coal, and coal reserves figures are also presented in this chapter.

In Chapter 9 the non-OPEC countries are presented, beginning with the United States. The 1956 theory of the geologist King M. Hubbert is explained; Hubbert predicted that oil would begin to run out — and sooner rather than later. Factors that contribute to the diminishing availability of oil are also presented: the declining productivity of fields already in production, for instance. North Sea producers, such as Great Britain and Norway, whose production is already clearly diminishing, Mexico, Russia and the former Soviet Union, the Caspian Sea and the situation in China are considered. And it is posited that the great competition of the new century will be centered on oil and the development of sources that can be substituted for it, an objective that has so far eluded us.

Chapter 10 looks at the OPEC countries, Algeria, Iran, Iraq, Kuwait, Libya, Nigeria, Qatar, Saudi Arabia, the United Arab Emirates and Venezuela.

This book strives to analyze the problem thoroughly, opposing all theses with their antitheses. Thus, in Chapter 11 the contrary vision is presented. There certainly exists a view that oil will not be used up but rather it will be replaced by other energy sources. Former Saudi oil minister Ahmed Yamani declared that oil would not disappear in 2001, but rather it will be replaced by other energy sources. "The Stone Age did not end because there were no more stones." We look at attempts to develop more energy-efficient technologies and alternative fuels.

Chapter 12 assesses how long the reserves may last and ponders the political and military consequences of a real oil crisis. It discusses the efforts made by automakers to develop hydrogen-fuel vehicles. The effects of either of the two scenarios — oil exhaustion or its replacement — on politics and the economy are considered. But this brings out the contradiction in one of the largest consumer sectors, the auto industry, which continues producing motors that run on leaded gasoline for the Third World countries in spite of the great environmental damage that is being done to the whole planet.

In Chapter 13, we take a historical view of how petroleum products have been used, from the first use of oil as a fuel for electric power generation and heating to gasoline and lubricants, and the role of oil in the past century's wars and more recent confrontations.

In Chapter 14, production figures and prices of oil are shown from its discovery in 1859 until the year 2000, glossed with comments on the main historical events and the possible effects that oil could have had on them; Chapter 15 presents some general conclusions.

Chapter 1. The New Paradigm

Up to now, it has been considered that the developed countries got that way because they had large volumes of capital to drive their economic, social, scientific and technological progress. And, conversely, that undeveloped countries are undeveloped because they do not have sufficient capital resources. The paradigm says that development is a consequence of capital accumulation and that it is not sufficient to have natural resources and a workforce.[2] This distortion has meant that capital was seen as an original factor of production, autonomous, a creator of wealth and not really what it is: a derived factor, the fruit of man's invention and a consequence of his action on nature. In other words, a society may have an abundance of natural resources and workforce for production, but will not get far on those assets alone because the decisive factor is capital. Further supporting this idea is a fact that up to now has been undisputed: the countries with the greatest abundance of natural resources and population are, indeed, the poorest and least developed.

But in the 21st century the situation will be different. And, indeed, it is already beginning to be different. Natural resources will be recognized as the most important factor of production, and it will become clear that they are the irreplaceable component in the wealth-generation process. This does not mean that capital will lose its importance as factor of production. Natural resources have always occupied a special place, because they are the original factor of production; but to the extent they have been abundant, their importance has not been

---

2. But the economy has not recognized sufficiently that the capital accumulation in the developed countries has its origin in the overexploitation of the natural resources and the overexploitation of human labor, in their own territories and, especially, in the Third World.

properly hierarchized and valued. The proof of this is the scant appreciation that mankind and the economy have shown for such indispensable items as water, oxygen and plants. But everything indicates that this trend — by force of circumstance — will soon shift and that humanity will have to place a far higher value on natural resources. There is no advantage in having modern machines, science and technology or having abundant money, if you do not have — in sufficiency — the resources that nature provides.

The shortage of resources will be a result of overexploitation and of the destruction of the environment through pollution. As fresh water and oxygen sources decrease, the forests and agricultural land suffer and shrink. Add to that the contamination of the seas, over fishing, wasteful use of nuclear energy and fossil fuels, all of which are generators of the greenhouse effect.

Man can develop new forms of capital, just as he has done up to now. Money is his invention and machines are, too. But man cannot replace nature in its creative role as supplier. If, due to overexploitation or the effects of pollution, natural resources begin to dry up, the complete structure on which the modern world was built will suffer major changes. The abundance or the lack of natural resources does not depend on man's will. Man can reach — and has reached — high production levels in agriculture under favorable natural conditions. But if those conditions disappear, due for example to the greenhouse effect, then man will not be able to repeat those achievements. The same applies to other productive and social activities. What happens with natural resources defines, in important ways, human life.

The shortage of natural resources because of exhaustion or as a consequence of predatory human action has not been considered as a global economic problem[3] because man always found ways to obtain more. When resources were depleted — as in the case of certain mines or forest or agricultural areas — man moved on, generally with success. But now, there is no place else to go. The availability of water is diminishing in many regions of the world because the cycle of nature has been disrupted; the forests where the rivers are born have been destroyed and pollution is increasing. Oxygen begins to be a very valuable consumer good in the big metropolises like Tokyo and Mexico City, which already have set up centers to supply oxygen to the population. In Sao Paulo and Rio de Janeiro, in Brazil, air pollution causes 4000 premature deaths per year.[4]

There are regions like Southwest Asia where a variety of plants that constituted the main source of food and medicines have been destroyed. The fish populations along the east coast of North America have almost disappeared and the Atlantic catch has diminished from 2.5 million tons in 1971 to less than 500,000 tons in 1994. The underground water supply in Western Asia is in a critical situ-

---

3. Pernaut, Manuel s.j. Teoría Económica. UCAB, Caracas, "There is no economic problem if the resources are plentiful," page 38, UCAB, Caracas, 1967.
4. Naciones Unidas. Informe Geo 2000.

ation because the volumes extracted exceed the rates of natural replacement. Arctic marine silts commonly present radioactive isotopes as a result of the radioactive precipitation coming from weapons tests in the atmosphere, military accidents and Europeans nuclear reprocessing plant discharges. If the current rules of consumption follow their course, in the year 2025 two out of three humans will live under stressful conditions because of the lack of water.[5]

"Desertification and drought affected 900 million people in a hundred countries in 2000 and it is considered that by 2025 this number will be doubled, and therefore 25% of the earth's surface will be degraded," says the World Bank.[6]

And the worst is still to come: a real energy crisis, because man is using up the resources of fossil energy, especially oil.

The signs enumerated above — and many others that are well known to the international bodies — demonstrate the Earth's diminishing capacity to furnish many of the resources that are indispensable for life in the quantities that are required to sustain economic growth and the modern patterns of consumption.

Short of a miracle, the non-negotiable shortage of resources will inexorably limit production. This will generate, necessarily, a new economy paradigm and will transform natural resources into the main economic problem of the century. It will determine, in turn, significant limitations in the possibilities of capital formation and of labor expansion, reinforcing the poverty cycle, in this case not because of the shortage of capital factor but of natural resources.

The oil crisis of 1973, when the Arab countries decided not to sell more oil to the United States, revealed a new world reality. If this decision made by a small group of countries precipitated the world into a crisis that affected the whole economy and changed international power relationships forever, one can only imagine what would happen if the contrary phenomenon took place, in other words, a reduction of the supply of oil worldwide, not as a result of political decisions but as a consequence of exhaustion at the source.

But reduced oil supplies are not the only problem. The supply of other vital resources is also being reduced. The great challenge for world leaders is to understand this reality and to adopt measures today that guarantee to future generations the possibility of continuing to live on this planet. If they fail to do so, the next generations will find themselves in a world where life can no longer be sustained.

The problem is complex. Pollution alone has reached a level that endangers many forms of life. How mankind can go forward is the greatest challenge facing political leaders and scientists alike. If, out of an excessive pragmatism, they only concentrate on the problems at hand, here and now, and fail to provide for the future, humanity as a whole will be under serious threat.

---

5. Ibid., pages 4, 7, 10, 11, 12.
6. World Report 1999-2000, page 88.

A NEW VISION OF THE FACTORS OF PRODUCTION

Until recently economic theory has not seriously considered that a global shortage of natural resources could occur, and even less a global shortage of water and petroleum. Neither economists nor political leaders nor the major media have seen beyond the appearance to comprehend the essence of the situation. Most people have not given much consideration to the possibility of the actual depletion of natural resources, on the assumption that it is a localized problem specific to certain regions of the world. Only when people come to recognize how widespread and how irremediable are these shortages will the whole analysis structure and perspective change.

Organizations like the FAO (Food and Agriculture Organization of the United Nations), for example, maintain a dual position in relation to the water supply. The institution does not express long-term concern in relation to a possible global shortage of water, but recognizes the droughts that occur in various regions of the world. But the position of OPEC (Organization of the Petroleum Exporting Countries) is even more significant. OPEC has not made any official announcement about the progressive depletion of the reserves and the increasing consumption of petroleum, though the combination of these two elements reveals clearly that this resource is on its way to exhaustion. There is a special omission, then, on the part of the most important international bodies in relation to a possible global scarcity of the two most important resources for life and production, water and petroleum.

Man has used raw materials without any limitation, those used directly in production and those that are essential to maintain life, such as air, fresh water, various nutrients and other basic elements. For this reason, and given the apparent abundant existence of resources, economic theory still has not seen the necessity of considering the scenario of an absolute scarcity of natural resources.

Historians consider that humanity's main steps forward were obtained in the period prior to the invention of written language. In that long stage, man created the first tools and discovered the elementary methods of production. He discovered fire, created the bow and arrow, he learned to manufacture garments from the skin of animals, and he discovered agriculture and tamed animals; he learned how to use leather and bone, and used stones to mill grain, created the plow, invented ceramics, learned how to use metals (first copper, later brass and then iron). Historians consider that the invention of the written language coincided with the discovery of how to smelt metals. The Historical Age begins at this point.

Man has always exercised dominion over the factors of production and with the passing of the time he has only been consolidating and improving that dominion. But starting with the second half of the 18th century — the Industrial Revolution — a great change took place in the scale and technologies of production with the invention of modern machines. Some of the most important innovations took place in the textiles field, with the creation of a system to improve fabric pieces in 1733, the mechanical spindle to automatically twist thread, in 1776, and the first mechanical looms in 1875. Advances in metallurgy were also significant, as the first steels were obtained in 1750, while in the energy field the first steam motors that would lead to steam-driven factory equipment were created in 1764. Since then, science and technology have achieved an ever faster pace of acceleration, giving rise to the development of a large-scale industry, the foundation of big industrial and mercantile cities and the consolidation of industrial capitalism.

In parallel to this great industrial development, the political economy also underwent a great development. In 1776, that is to say, twelve years after the steam engine was created, Adam Smith published his work, "Research on the nature and causes of the wealth of the nations." In it, Adam Smith outlines the formal division of the factors of production as capital, earth and labor. Political economy took on a new dimension. But Smith was not the first intellectual to study the economic problem so thoroughly. The ancient Greeks were the ones who created the term "economy," which was translated as running the house or domestic economy.

The Industrial Revolution should really be called the Energy Revolution, because the great change in the form of production had it origin, in fact, in the invention of the steam engine that was incorporated into the manufacturing and transportation industries, creating a new scale of production and increasing the speed at which people and goods were transported, through the railroads and the new steam ships which invigorated trade and industry.

The Industrial Revolution certainly represented a radical change. In the brief span from the middle of the 18th century to the early 21st century, humanity went from a rural and circumscribed way of life to the largely urbanized and internationalized culture we know today, due to specific major inventions — may of which are directly linked to the use of petroleum products. The Industrial Revolution brought a change in the form of the uses of the factors of production because, as a consequence of the victory of industrial capitalism first and the emergence of financial capitalism after, the most important factor of production has been capital. (That included, besides money, all the elements that contribute to production — all man-made aids to production — such as buildings, machinery, transportation means and also know-how.)

The new scale of production created by the scientific and technological progress allowed a more efficient use of natural resources and of human labor, and although it certainly demanded more natural resources as the market expanded, it is also certain that economic theorists found no reason to worry about a possible scarcity of natural resources. New sources could always be found. Adam Smith recognized the limitation of the factors of production but he did not consider that limitation to be an obstacle that would impede the realization of economic activities. When he distinguished among the concepts of wages, benefits and rent, he accepted that the factors were scarce and, consequently, they should receive remuneration. The distribution of scarce resources has been the paradigm of the economy.

FROM MALTHUS TO THE CLUB OF ROME

But in 1798 Thomas Robert Malthus (1776-1834) published *An Essay on the Principle of Population.*[7]

> [P]opulation, when unchecked, goes on doubling itself every twenty-five years, or increases in a geometrical ratio. The rate according to which the productions of the earth may suppose to be increased, it will not be so easy to determine. Out of this, however, we may be perfectly certain, that the ratio of its increase in a limited territory must be of a totally different nature from the ratio of the increase of population. A billion are just as easily doubled every twenty-five years by the power of population as a thousand. But the food to support the increase from the greater number will by no means be obtained with the same facility.[8]... It may be fairly pronounced, therefore, that, considering the present average state of the earth, the means of subsistence, under circumstances the most favorable to human industry, could not possibly be made to increase faster than in an arithmetical ratio.[9]

Malthus was harshly criticized as an economist but he drew attention to the important idea that demographic growth represents an absolute limitation on economic growth or, at least, it acts as a brake on growth.

Malthus could not have foreseen the green revolution and biotechnological innovation that enabled mankind in the 20th century to boost production to levels unthinkable in the 19th century. However, and in spite of the increase in agricultural production, humanity still has not been able to escape the specter of hunger. And the outlook is even more desperate for the 21st century because all the indicators point to a serious worldwide shortage of a wide range of resources.

Many years later, another work in economic theory attracted attention to the issue. "The Limits to Growth" was produced by a group of scientists from the Massachusetts Technological Institute (MIT) between 1968 and 1972, for the Club of Rome. The purpose of the work was to research humanity's long-term outlook and to that end a model with 69 variables was built. The main variables were population, food supply, nonrenewable natural resources, capital and pollution. The study concluded that if demographic growth, the pattern of consumption and the effective levels of pollution stayed at the same rate as in the early 1970s, the population of the world would reach a maximum by the middle of the 21st century. After that, it would drop precipitously due to scarcity of food

---

7. Malthus, Thomas Robert. *An essay on the principle of population*, Book I, page 5. J.M. Dent & Sons LTD, London. 1933.
8. Ibid., page 8.
9. Ibid., page 10.

and natural resources, plus pollution. The study generated discussion in the following years, but its conclusions were later watered down and then buried.

In 1970, while the researchers at MIT were in the heat of their work, the first signs of what would be the first great oil crisis became visible. The Libyan leader Muammar Gadafi began putting pressure on the oil companies to raise the price of petroleum. This was the prelude to the oil crisis of 1974 and it should have contributed to the dawning recognition of society's vulnerability to the shortfall in natural resources that MIT had already elaborated in its report.

THE LEONTIEF THESIS

In 1977, *The Future of the World Economy* was published by the United Nations. The work of Nobel Laureate in Economics Wassily Leontief and other economists, the report contradicted the predictions of the Club of Rome; it presented an optimistic view on the physical and environmental potential of the future and it asserted that the limits on growth are not physical but rather of political, social and institutional nature. The study affirmed that although pollution is a serious problem for humanity, it constitutes a technologically controllable problem since the economic cost of keeping pollution within manageable limits is not unattainable, that is to say that "the problem of pollution and of the fight against it does not constitute an insurmountable barrier for rapid development."[10]

Economic Theory and the Lack of Interest in Natural Resources

In 1979, two years after the Leontief report came the work of Professors P.S. Dasgupta of the London School of Economics and G.M. Heal of the University of Sussex, who noted that in all the considerable developments in economic theory in the twentieth century, there was little explicit mention of natural resources.[11] "The lack of direct reference to resources in this literature presumably reflects the fact that for the first two-thirds of the twentieth century, resource constraints were not important for most industrialized nations; these either possessed their own resources supplies, which they regarded as adequate, or felt that they could be confident of importing resources in unlimited amounts from developing countries." Professors Dasgupta and Heal note that in the last quarter of the twentieth century the situation changed and the situation as regards natural resources became a major interest, highlighted in Forrester's book *World Dynamics* and in publications of the Club of Rome.

10. Leontief, Wassily. *El futuro de la economía mundial*, pp. 30-31. Editorial Akal, Madrid, 1977.
11. Dasgupta P.S. and Heal G.M. *Economic theory and exhaustible resources*, p. 1. Cambridge University Press. 1979.

By the middle of the 1980s, a new analytical perspective took hold: the goal of sustainable development. In the last several decades political and institutional efforts have been made to protect the environment. The most remarkable is the Kyoto Protocol, the main objective of which is to secure cooperation worldwide to reduce the adverse effects of contamination and to guarantee the sustainable development. The US lacks the political will to implement the measures called for, and pulled out of the agreement, saying it would be too costly. In spite of all these intellectual and political efforts, the deterioration of the environment and the depletion of natural resources continue at an unchecked pace.

SIGNS OF SHORTAGE

Water has already begun to be scarce in many parts of the world, especially in the most populated areas. The crisis is already real in nations like China and India. The shortage of water has as logical results in a crisis of food supply and of industrial and services production because water is the basic input. In the Report World Development 2003, the World Bank affirms that "Fresh water consumption is rising quickly, and the availability of water in some regions is likely to become one of the most pressing issues of the 21st century. One-third of the world's population lives in countries that are already experiencing a moderate to sharp water shortage. That proportion could (at current population forecasts) rise to half or more in the next 30 years unless institutions change to ensure better conservation and allocation of water. More than a billion people in low- and middle-income countries — and 50 million people in high-income countries — lack access to safe drinking water, and water for personal hygiene, and domestic use."[12]

CONCLUSION

Since the publication of Thomas Robert Malthus's essay in 1798, little outstanding economics research has been conducted regarding natural resources. The 19th century had its David Ricardo and John Stuart Mill. The last 35 years saw the MIT work for the Club of Rome, published in 1972, Wassily Leontief's 1977 work for the United Nations, the 1979 thesis of P.S. Dasgupta and G.M. Heal, of the London School of Economics, and the World Bank's writings on sustainable development. In the 1980s, the Matrix of Social Accounting gave us a better understanding of the structural interdependences of the economy.

In conclusion, one can say that the world is so confident in the abundance of natural resources that no one has seriously contemplated any other possibility and

---

12. World Bank, World Development Report 2003, *Sustainable development in a dynamic world*, page 2. Washington. 2003.

its consequences for humanity. This book does establish that possibility. If the supply is insufficient or nonexistent, production cannot be carried out or must at least be limited. Demand for factors of production has already outstripped their supply. This is more than an economic problem, and it must be addressed at all levels of society.

With the arrival of the new millennium, the world has entered a very difficult situation, well-known in its details only to a very few specialists: it is the beginning of the end of the oil era.

CHAPTER 2. ECONOMY, ENERGY AND THE ENVIRONMENT

Man produces things with a defined purpose: to satisfy his needs. And his needs grow as he reaches new goals and develops his creative capacity. The population consumes the production. One might say, then, that population growth generates new production and consumption needs. But in reality, in ordinary life, the situation is different. Need is one thing and the capacity to satisfy that need is another. A society can have many needs but it may have no, or a limited, capacity to satisfy them. That is what has happened up to now. A potential demand for consumer goods has been generated and, consequently, for raw material, for inputs and for machinery to satisfy the new needs derived from the population's growth. But due to the poverty that most of the world lives in, that growth in global demand has not become effective demand on a scale that corresponds with the population's growth.

Only a small part of that new population has much impact on demand worldwide. North America, Japan and Western Europe represented only approximately 10% of the world population in 1999, but they had achieved the highest level in satisfaction of economic and social needs up to that point. The rest of the world is poor, mostly on the verge of subsistence. Only 23 countries have high revenues, that is to say, an income greater than $9,266 annual per capita; they concentrated 80% of the world income in 1999. These countries are Australia, Austria, Belgium, Canada, Hong Kong, Denmark, Finland, France, Germany, Greece, Ireland, Israel, Italy, Japan, Holland, Norway, Portugal, Singapore, Spain, Sweden, Switzerland, United Kingdom and the United States. The other 126 countries of the world have less than $2,955 annual per capita — and they only receive 20% of the world income.

Table 1. High Income Countries* National Income Per Capita. 1999.

Country	$
Switzerland	38,380
Norway	33,470
Denmark	32,050
Japan	32,030
United States	31,910
Sweden	26,750
Germany	25,620
Austria	25,430
Holland	25,140
Finland	24,730
Belgium	24,650
Hong Kong	24,570
France	24,170
Singapore	24,150
United Kingdom	23,590
Ireland	21,470
Australia	20,950
Italy	20,170
Canada	20,140
Israel	16,310
Spain	14,800
Greece	12,110
Portugal	11,030

Over time, the high-income countries tend to bring in more and more of the world revenues and, conversely, the share left to the low- and middle-income countries tends to diminish.

Table 2. Gross National Income. 1999 and 2003.

	$ Billions (1999)	% (1999)	$ Billions (2003)	% (2003)
Total world	29,995	100	34,577	100
Low income countries (a)	1,008	3.4	1,021	2.95
Medium income countries (b)	5,285	17.6	5,756	16.64
High income countries (c)	23,702	79.0	27,806	80.41

(a) $755 or less annual per capita income
(b) $756 -$9,265
(c) $9,266 or more.
Source: World Bank, 2001 World Development Indicators, page 14, and World Bank, 2005 World Development Indicators, page 24.

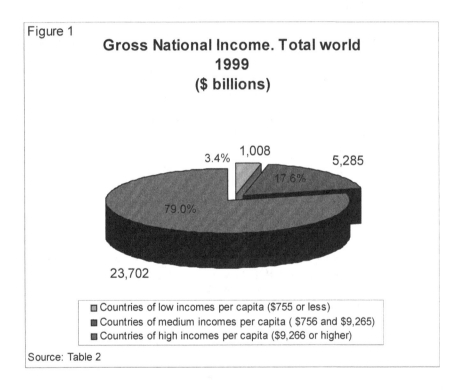

Figure 1

**Gross National Income. Total world
1999
($ billions)**

3.4% 1,008   5,285

17.6%

79.0%

23,702

■ Countries of low incomes per capita ($755 or less)
■ Countries of medium incomes per capita ($756 and $9,265)
■ Countries of high incomes per capita ($9,266 or higher)

Source: Table 2

EFFECTS OF THE WORLD INCOME DISTRIBUTION

Population growth in the developed countries has not had the same effect on global demand as population growth in the Third World countries. The high

19

growth of Third World population has not had a very significant impact on demand; on the contrary, the moderate rate of population growth in the developed countries has caused the most significant changes in demand worldwide.

The United States, for example, with barely 278 million inhabitants in 1999 (4.65% of the world's population, 5,978 million people in 1999[13]) was the leading consumer of oil, at 18.7 million barrels/day for 2000. Japan, with just 2.12% of world population, was in second place, consuming 5.5 million barrels of oil daily. China, with a whopping 21% of the world population, ranked third, consuming 4.8 million barrels/day. Germany, with only 1.37% of the population, came in fourth with 2.7 million barrels a day. And Russia, with 2.44% of the world population, was fifth with 2.4 million barrels/day.[14] This means that the United States population consumes more oil than Japan, China, Germany, Russia, South Korea and India all together and the United States is the biggest individual oil consumer in the world.

But this trend could change significantly in the next few years. For example, studies of worldwide demand for oil indicate that regions that had been at the margins of development until 2001, especially in Latin America and Asia, are now consuming more oil and will consume much more in the near future, given that, among other causes, a very significant part of the transnational industries have moved to these countries. In recent years the developed world has been transferring to the Third World part of its industrial structure, because these countries impose fewer regulations in regard to protecting the environment (and the workers). The general structure of costs and wages is smaller than in the developed countries.

THE NEW REALITY OF THE WORLD ECONOMY

The world economy has two major points of vulnerability: natural population growth and the new demand derived from the incorporation into the labor market of a large segment of the population of the Third World countries.

One must also consider the efforts of Third World countries to expand their economies with their own resources, generating a new possibility for world economic expansion. But the expansion of the economy depends on one factor on which man has very little influence: natural resources. Are there sufficient natural resources in the world to fulfill the demand that stems from the population's growth and the increasing consumer expectations created by the economic expansion of both the industrialized countries and those of the Third World countries?

---

13. World Bank 2001 *World Development Indicators*, page 46.
14. B.P. Statistical Review of World Energy 2001.

If, in satisfying the needs of only 10% of the world population, our natural resources show signs of depletion, it is logical to ask what would happen if a small part of the remaining 90% of the world's population got their share. How can we raise the standard of living in the poorest Asia and African countries to equal in material terms the standard of living in the rich Western countries? How much oil would it take to feed the Chinese population's automobiles if they used them like Americans?

THE NEW RESTRICTIVE FACTOR OF ECONOMIC GROWTH

If a world economic expansion should bring along the countries that have lagged behind in the development process, the rate at which the natural resources would be exhausted would be vastly accelerated. The global crisis in natural resources will very soon be felt if the industrialized countries maintain the average rate of the economic growth and if even a very small expansion takes place in the economy of the countries of the Third World.

The environmental implications are enormous. If the present production pattern persists, with its intense use of the most polluting energy sources, environmental destruction will also accelerate.

The growth of wealth in the industrialized nations has been possible thanks to the exploitation of natural resources in their own territories and in the rest of the world and especially the unlimited exploitation of energy sources, first wood, then coal, and since 1860, oil. But that pattern has reached a crisis point because some natural resources are already running out and pollution is reaching unsustainable levels. Every day the lack of water is more evident. Restrictions on the use of electricity and on the use of fuels are tighter and tighter in various regions of the world and are already part of everyday life. And those shortages and restrictions will only be amplified in the future.

LIMITS OF ECONOMIC GROWTH

In the developed countries, economic growth is stimulated by advertising because most of the population has already had its basic needs met. That does not mean that poverty does not exist in the highly developed countries. Poor sectors exist, but in a very different form than in the Third World. In the developed countries, the poor receive services and subsistence incomes through social security systems that the poor populations in most Third World countries do not have. In the developed countries, consumerism is the force that moves the economy. Some people change their car every year. They can't be bothered to have appliances repaired. The economic structure of the developed countries is built to favor intense consumption. One of the basic goals of the financial broker in these countries is to increase consumption. In poor countries, few people buy automobiles and they make them last for decades.

Looking at it from the production side, economic growth, that is the net accumulation of capital, requires first that the factors of production exist in sufficient quantity. If any of the factors fails, then there cannot be growth, or it will be limited at best. A limit is imposed by the shortage of any of the factors of production or by a combination of them. The scarcity and deterioration of natural resources will reinforce the existing growth pattern, that is, the concentration of wealth in the developed nations. It will be very difficult for any nation — developed or undeveloped — to consistently raise its standard of living. Moreover, it might become hard even to maintain the nation's economic status; replacement investments might be in danger, even for developed nations. Not only will growth be limited, but standards may well drop. If the scarcity of drinking water becomes more widespread, if air pollution intensifies, if the disposal of garbage and toxic waste becomes unmanageable, we are all in trouble.

In addition to the limits cited above, there are growth limits inherent in the size of any nation's domestic economy. To exceed those limits, new markets have to be found outside. For rich countries, it is harder to find new markets for their products; rich countries with similar characteristics generally are competing with each other and their populations' needs are, to a greater or lesser degree, equally satisfied.

THE THIRD WORLD IS THE POTENTIAL MARKET

Consequently, the countries of the Third World, which confront all types of necessities, appear to represent the most promising new markets; but they do not have enough money to acquire goods in the international market. These countries are mostly producers of raw materials; for the most part, they have little to offer in exchange for processed goods and services. Some perform the role of assemblers, assigned to them by the international division of labor imposed by the big transnational corporations. The Third World as a potential market theoretically could make possible a major expansion of the world economy, but that potential market is limited by several circumstances: a) small purchasing capacity due to their dependence (in good measure) on international loans to support their imports; b) their high level of debt, which subtracts resources from their domestic markets and diverts foreign currency revenues to interest payments, and c) the greatest restriction of all: the shortage of natural resources, which is already becoming evident.

FULL EMPLOYMENT IS UNATTAINABLE ON A GLOBAL SCALE

There may be partial successes in the areas of job creation and economic expansion, especially in those countries that receive the largest investments from the First World. But full employment (as we currently conceive it) in every country of the world is going to be hard to achieve, because there simply are not enough natural resources to sustain it. And as the economic expansion of the high-income countries grows, unemployment and poverty in the low-income countries is only more irremediably cast in stone. The economic expansion of one or several regions of the world will be always at the expense of other, bigger regions. North American and Western European expansion has been supported by the exploitation of Latin America, Asia, Oceania and African, regions that have given the natural resources, the raw material and the workforce, most of the time in slave labor. The more recent economic expansion of countries like China, too, is a consequence of the intense exploitation of the natural resources of their neighbors and others, including the Middle East, which has been supplying China with oil. In the year 2000, China produced 3,000,245 barrels of oil per day and consumed 4,840,000 barrels/day. This deficit of 1,839,755 barrels/day, representing 61% of their domestic production, must be imported. So to maintain its economic expansion rate, China — whose particular situation deserves mention because it has the largest population in the world — will accelerate the use of energy, especially of oil. Where will China get the fast-growing supply that its economy will demand in the future?

In order to enable Third World countries to buy the products of the First World countries, the international financial system has designed diverse forms of financial credit, which quickly become impossible to repay and that transforms the poorest countries into modern vassals. "I lend to you so that you keep buying from me." And as you cannot pay me back, I encourage you to keep borrowing and I keep on selling to you. This eternal debt is impossible to pay off. For example, after years of crisis, in the last days of December 2001, Argentina, one of the largest economies of Latin America, was declared unable to pay its foreign debt of more than $141 billion, after bloody disturbances that brought down the government. Argentina is a good example of a country that racked up foreign debt and applied politics that had been successful in the developed countries but that were not adapted to the Argentinean reality. The result has been a total crash.

Third World countries are *all* in debt. Brazil had the largest foreign debt in the world for 2003, with $235,431,000,000. China is next, with $193,567,000,000, Russia with $175,257,000,000, and Argentina with $166,207,000,000. The following table shows how foreign debt is distributed among the countries of the world, except Oceania.

The debt has grown dramatically between 1990 and 2003. Brazil, for example, doubled its debt, Argentina almost tripled its debt, and China almost quadrupled its debt. This phenomenon may be observed in the rest of the countries as well, as shown in Table 3.

Table 3. Total External Debt in $ Millions. Top 20 Countries.

Country	1990	2003
Brazil	119,965	235,431
China	55,301	193,567
Russia	—	175,257
Argentina	62,233	166,207
Turkey	49,424	145,662
Mexico	104,442	140,004
Indonesia	69,872	134,389
India	83,628	113,467
Poland	49,364	95,219
Philippines	30,580	62,663
Thailand	28,095	51,793
Malaysia	15,328	49,074
Hungary	21,202	45,785
Chile	19,226	43,231
Pakistan	20,663	36,345
Nigeria	33,439	34,963
Venezuela	33,171	34,851
Czech Republic	—	34,630
Colombia	17,222	32,979
Egypt	33,017	31,383

Source World Bank. World Development Indicators 2005. Pages 258-260.

DEBT: THE NEW REGULATOR OF THE ECONOMY

Foreign debt is a new tool used by creditors to keep the economy going in a certain way. That poverty levels in the world remain fixed is a consequence, among other causes, of this situation. If the creditors are interested in a greater expansion of the world economy at a certain moment, they increase their loans to the undeveloped countries and ease the payment terms and reduce interest rates. But if, on the contrary, they want to keep the economy at a certain state or bring it down due to a specific economic situation, then they do the opposite; they tighten the rules, they make it harder for undeveloped countries to get new loans, and they get tough about collecting pending debt; so that the undeveloped countries' foreign debt is the new regulator mechanism for world economy growth.

The world market grows not only because of demand from the rich nations but because of the unsatisfied demand from the poor nations, demand that is satisfied in a good part with the loans obtained from the international financial system.

The trade figures for high-income countries, members of the OECD (Organization for Economic Cooperation and Develop) and the low- and medium-income countries reveal the changes in the flow of imports and exports at the end of the 20th century.

Table 4. OECD Members' Imports from Low- and Medium-Income Countries

Imports ($ billions)	1990	1999
Foods	64.2	94.1
Cereals	1.3	2.4
Agriculture and raw materials	17.3	22.1
Minerals and non ferrous metals	30.1	42.7
Fuels	144.2	139.8
Crude oil	107.5	100.7
Oil products	23.5	21.9
Manufactured goods	208.3	667.8
Chemical products	14.0	30.6
Machinery and transport equipment	59.1	292.0
Others	135.2	345.1
Miscellaneous goods	5.5	12.5
Total	469.7	979.0

Source: World Bank. 2001 World Development Indicators. Page 328.

The total OECD member countries imports from low- and medium-income countries were increased by 108% between 1990 and 1999, from $469.7 billion to $979 billion. Total OECD exports toward Third World low and- medium income countries increased by 88% during the same period, from $378.5 to $712.9 billion.

Table 5. OECD Members' Exports to Low- and Medium-Income Countries

Exports ($ billions)	1990	1999
Foods	34.1	52.3
Cereals	14.0	13.8
Agriculture and raw materials	11.6	14.3
Minerals and non ferrous metals	9.3	14.9
Fuels	8.5	14.2
Crude oil	0.3	1.8
Oil products	5.6	8.9
Manufactured goods	303.4	593.4
Chemical products	45.4	81.2
Machinery and transport equipment	174.5	349.1
Others	83.6	163.1
Miscellaneous goods	11.6	23.8
Total	378.5	712.9

Source: World Bank. 2001 World Development Indicators. Page 327.

There is a seemingly positive balance in favor of low-income countries. In 1990, OECD countries imported $208.3 billion in manufactured goods from low-income countries; in 1999 that figure tripled, to $667.8 billion. Theoretically, that would suggest that the Third World is attaining a more and more important position in the world economy, and that would be tied to increased fuel consumption in those countries and especially the increase of oil consumption in recent years, a trend that seems likely to be accentuated in the years ahead.

The world trade figures reveal a change in the structure of this trade, as the poor countries increase their capacity for the production of manufactured goods. But what is the true social and economic impact of that change? Are the production activities that are carried out in the Third World countries really "production," or are these only false industries, assembling industries, "maquila" industries as they have been called? What is the environmental effect of the growth in Third World industrial capacity?

The intense exploitation of natural resources will be the distinctive characteristic of this expansion process, which is following the "Enclave Pattern" of development exemplified by the United Fruit Company as it converted much of the Americas into a series of "banana republics." Now, in addition to agricultural interests, the big transnational companies are transferring part of their manufacturing and assembling activities toward those countries to take advantage of the natural resources and the cheap manpower.

CHANGES IN THE POPULATION'S STRUCTURE

While the percentage of young people in the population of developed nations is shrinking and life expectancy is rising — a phenomenon known as "Demographic Transition" — in poor countries, the contrary is happening; they are experiencing an increase in birthrate and in mortality, so that the average age is far lower. Africa, for example, has tripled its population between 1950 and 1996, from 224 million to 739 million inhabitants. Latin America has grown similarly in the same period, from 166 million to 484 million inhabitants. Asia has more than doubled, from 1,402 to 3,488 million. Oceania, too, grew from 12.6 to 28.7 million. North America's population increase was something less than double, from 172 to 299 million. And Europe experienced the smallest rate of growth in that period, going from 547 to 729 million inhabitants.

Table 6. Population by Continents. 1950-1996.

	1950	1960	1970	1980	1985	1990	1995	1996
Africa	224	282	364	476	548	629	719	739
North America	172	204	232	255	268	282	297	299
Latin America	166	217	2.844	359	398	438	477	484
Asia	1.402	1.702	2.147	2.641	2.902	3.184	3.438	3.488
Europe	547	605	656	693	707	722	728	729
Oceania	13	16	19	23	25	26	28	29
Total World	2,524	3,027	3,702	4,447	4,847	5,282	5,687	5,768

Source: United Nations. Statistical Yearbook, 43rd issue, New York, 1999.
Dates available to 30 September 1998.

THE NEW ECONOMIC PARADIGM

The economy of the 21st century is the economy of the distribution of the scarce resources. The paradigm has supposed — until now — the abundance of natural resources (the land factor) and of the labor factor. The paradigm has considered that the scarce factor of production has always been capital, in its currency form or in its technology and goods for production form. And, indeed, man has enjoyed an abundance of natural resources and of manpower, but has used them to lavish goods upon just 10% of the world population.

When 90% of the population have eked by on very little, the demands on nature were limited. But now, the 90% are more aware of the outside world, and they want their share. The economy will have to face a new paradigm. By the intense use of capital resources to boost production, we are quickly exhausting the supply of unreplaceable materials.

What will we do without fresh water? Rationing has already pitted residential areas against farmers in California and elsewere. Efficient and affordable methods of purifying and desalinating water on a massive scale have yet to be found; neither have the attempts to find new sources of energy come up with a substitute for petroleum products. Science and technology must be directed to finding the most efficient ways to use the resources we have, but neither science nor technology can replace the vital resources.

THE EQUATION OF MODERNITY

The development pattern followed thus far has relied on an ever-increasing use of fuel and other inputs. The result is logical:

$$\Delta \text{ Population } \Delta \text{ Energy consumption } \Delta \text{ Pollution} =$$
$$\nabla \text{ Oil } \nabla \text{ Forests } \nabla \text{ Water } \nabla \text{ Food } \Delta \text{ Illnesses}$$

Now, humanity's great challenge is to manage economic growth and generate employment while using clean energy, non-pollutant energy — or the least polluting possible, so that we can arrive at a pattern more like:

$$\Delta \text{ Economic growth} = \nabla \text{ Contamination}$$

However, clean energy sources like water (hydroelectric power) are in diminishing supply and the other fuels, such as coal and nuclear energy, are highly polluting and dangerous. Natural gas is dangerous on a smaller scale. Efforts to develop new energy sources like eolic, solar energy, hydrogen and others, have not been able to replace oil and coal.

Before the great industrial development, the equation was different:

$$\Delta \text{ Population } \nabla \text{ Foods} = \Delta \text{ Illnesses}$$

Wood used to satisfy much of man's fuel needs, and great swathes of forests were razed. Illumination was obtained from vegetable oil or from whale's oil, or beeswax candles. And the needs of agriculture were fulfilled by windmills and by beasts of burden. Chemical contamination was practically nonexistent. And there was enough water to go around.

With the use of coal as a fuel, air pollution began to be a problem and with the advent of the oil era and the nuclear era, contamination reached a new high. Unless some new breakthrough occurs very soon, nuclear power will have greater and greater appeal; if no alternative is found, the risks will have to be ignored. But once developed, it is practically difficult to get rid of nuclear substances, and the hazards are profound.

CHAPTER 3. POPULATION AND ENERGY

ENERGY CONSUMPTION ALWAYS GROWS

As was observed in the previous chapter, the growing world population creates new production needs, but it does not necessarily generate effective demand for capital goods, intermediate goods nor consumer goods; the proof is the poor countries, whose populations are constantly increasing but who cannot raise their levels of consumption. Population growth is felt in terms of global demand only when the population has the means to pay: purchasing power, money to buy in the international markets. On the other hand, humans, wherever they live and whether or not they have purchasing power, always find some way to obtain some kind of energy. Even in the farthest reaches and most technologically backward places on the planet man uses some kind of fuel, if only in the most rudimentary way when he lights a fire. So that population growth automatically generates pressure on the energy sources: biomass, wood, coal, oil and other alternatives.

And using energy sources generates pollution, especially when it comes to fossil fuels such as oil, coal and natural gas (which represented more than 90% of the world's energy consumption in 1999). As a consequence, pollution is inevitable, and directly linked to population growth. And because population constantly grows, the production of energy is also constantly growing.

One common factor correlates natural resources, the economy and the environment: that common factor is the population of the world, which is growing every day, especially in the poorest regions. Between 1996 and 1997, the population of the world was increased by 121 million people, from 5.747 billion to 5.868 billions[15] (2.10%). When we correlate population growth with the avail-

---

15. Energy Information Administration, *International Energy Outlook 2000*, page 186.

ability of oil, water and food and with increased pollution, shortages must be inevitable.

That we are heading toward the exhaustion of crucial natural resources, "renewable" as they may be, is proven by the ongoing loss of species through extinction. How much more imminent must be the loss of nonrenewable resources? Oil can be used up. It can also be demonstrated that every day the quantity and quality of water and food available to meet the world's needs are going down and that this situation has it origin, essentially, in man's predatory attitude.

A METHODOLOGICAL CONCLUSION

Deductive reasoning leads to the obvious logical conclusion that finite resources like oil cannot last forever. However, there is a sense in many quarters that the supply is virtually inexhaustible, that new reserves are always being found, that there will be more than enough for the next few generations, and then — well, by then, man will have cleverly hit upon some other solution to his energy needs. But analysts who have studied the topic and geologists who have observed in practice how production is being increased and how the known reserves aer diminishing, have concluded that our oil reserves truly can be pumped dry, and in the not-too-distant future.

The deductive method impels us to accept as a basic premise that oil will be used up in a certain amount of time if humanity continues to use it. But if it would be helpful to consider the topic more thoroughly, to examine every nuance, let us go through a few scenarios:

A. A certain quantity of oil reserves have been discovered and proven in the world; it is perfectly possible that other small, equal or bigger reserves remain to be discovered.

B. Furthermore, those as yet undiscovered reserves could be smaller, equal to or greater than all the quantity discovered since the beginning of oil exploitation. Sophisticated technologies have enabled exploration and drilling offshore and in other sites that used to be inaccessible.

C. A third alternative would be that, indeed, the proven reserves currently acknowledged in the world might really be unique, or close to it, and there may be no other significant reserves that could be practically exploited.

These different scenarios each imply a different deadline but, in any case, all the usable oil will end up being depleted.

At the Twelfth World Petroleum Congress in Houston (1987) the nomenclatures to classify existing oil reserves were established. The categories were: proven reserves, proven reserves in development, proven reserves not developed, not proven reserves, probable reserves, possible reserves, and potential non discovered reserves.

The verifiable hypothesis today, the hypothesis with a real scientific basis, is that there are reserves located in various parts of the planet that modern prospecting methods have recognized as proven — and those are reflected in the petroleum statistics of international organizations. The existence of larger reserves — probable, possible and potential — corresponds to a hypothesis formulated on the base of certain scientific postulates, but it does not constitute a full test and remains therefore a matter of speculation. Those hypotheses may be correct. So, in accordance with the scientific method, which cannot be closed to any possibility, we shall leave that possibility on the table.

Still, the certain fact today is that the extent of the proven reserves have remained static in the last fifteen years. But more and more oil is being produced and consumed every day, and that will continue, as long as the oil holds out.

CHAPTER 4. RUNNING OUT OF OIL

EFFECTS OF THE OIL CRISIS

While the man on the street may find it unimaginable, many geologists and other researchers take it as an article of faith that we are running out of oil. The truth is too frightening to share with the public. The prices of oil and oil derivatives, and especially gasoline and lubricants, would shoot to unthinkable levels and production would be curtailed. Fierce speculation and hoarding would immediately take hold. In effect, the entire world would be catapulted into an economy war. The transport section would grind to a near halt. And, consequently, the distribution of food and other basic products would be seriously affected.

In an article entitled, "How Much Oil and Gas is Left?," the Society of Petroleum Engineers explains:

> Oil and gas exist in the pore spaces of rock in the subsurface of the earth. How much oil or gas can be recovered from the rock is a function of rock properties, technology, and economics. Even when it is technically feasible to remove oil or gas from a specific reservoir, the costs involved in doing so may exceed the value of the oil or gas recovered at projected prices. In this case, the oil or gas is uneconomic and will not be developed. As the price of a barrel goes up, the definition of what is "uneconomic" changes and oil companies are willing to work harder to get at even low-quality reserves. But even that scenario gives rise to a spiral of higher and higher costs and shorter and shorter supplies. The result is the same, only the time-frame shifts a little."[16]

---

16. Article dated August 23, 2005, accessed September 20, 2005, at http://www.spe.org/spe/jsp/basic_pf/0,,1104_1008218_1109511,00.html

Table 7. Consumption of Energy Worldwide. 1999.

Source of Energy	Million tons	% of World Total
Oil	3,462	40.6
Natural gas	2,064	24.2
Coal	2,130	25.0
Nuclear energy	651	7.6
Hydroelectric energy	227	2.6
Total World	8,533	100.0

Source: B.P. Statistical Review 2000.

Oil supplies 40% of the world's energy needs. A real oil crisis would indeed beat any Hollywood disaster scene. It is a problem of multiple implications. Economic growth is linked to oil consumption growth. If growth diminishes, the economies won't be able to generate jobs for the new generations. A recession feedback loop would ensue that could not be broken without elevating oil consumption.

What a paradox: to maintain economic growth, we have to consume more oil. But the more oil is consumed, the sooner it will run out.

In turn, as the gravity of the problem sinks in, prices will skyrocket until they reflect the value of petroleum's scarcity. Hyper inflation will cause world trade to contract. Economic growth will be a dream long gone.

As of 1999, coal was contributing 25% of the global energy while oil contributed 40.6%, as shown in Figure 2. The world depends of fossil fuels; and that has important social and environmental repercussions.

Fossil fuels are the main cause of the greenhouse effect. The options for reducing the use of fossil fuels are very limited and, at the same time, official projections forecast an escalation of their use in the next several years. This is a serious dilemma that humanity has not faced before. The world cannot stop satisfying its energy needs, but if continues down this path, in a few years a good part of the world's life will have disappeared.

Journalism students are taught early on that the public is generally not interested in what might happen far in the future, nor in what happens in faraway places. However, the satellite-delivered media have made the world smaller and now everybody can understand the effects of a phenomenon foreseen for the future. The world has not yet reacted to the imminent exhaustion of oil. But when that reality is recognized, there will be a cataclysm. And by then, perhaps it will be already too late. Meanwhile, politicians and global leaders dare not speak plainly about the danger; and since they cannot speak plainly, the world is not doing anything significant to diminish the demand for petroleum. The producers are obliged to increase supplies, when the reasonable thing would be to begin to radically decrease consumption and to conserve the resource. A parent should not

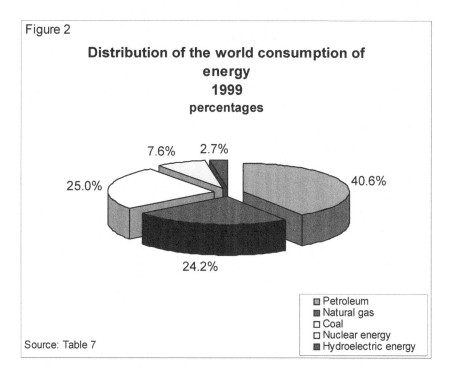

Figure 2

Distribution of the world consumption of energy 1999 percentages

7.6% 2.7%

25.0%

40.6%

24.2%

- Petroleum
- Natural gas
- Coal
- Nuclear energy
- Hydroelectric energy

Source: Table 7

spend all he has without thinking of his children's future. The current generation should not continue spending the oil that is left in the world without thinking of future generations.

The option of increasing oil consumption to maintain economic growth and to create employment, meeting society's current demands, generates yet another and no less serious problem, since the consumption of oil increases the emissions of polluting gases in the atmosphere that destroy the ozone layer.

Table 8. Countries Generating the Most Carbon Dioxide, in Metric Tons.

Country	1980	1996	% Change 1980-1996
United States	4,575	5,301	15.9
China	1,477	3,364	127.7
Russia	—	1,580	—
Japan	920	1,168	26.9
India	347	997	187.2
Germany	—	861	—
United Kingdom	584	557	-4.6
South Korea	125	408	226.0
Italy	372	403	8.4
France	483	362	-25.0
Mexico	252	348	38.4
Australia	203	307	51.2
Brazil	183	273	49.1
Saudi Arabia	131	268	104.9
Iran	116	267	129.7
North Korea	125	254	103.6
Indonesia	95	245	159.1
Thailand	40	205	413.5
Argentina	108	130	20.8
Venezuela	90	115	27.8
Egypt	45	98	116.6
Colombia	40	65	64.1
Chile	28	49	74.9

Source: World Bank. 2000 World Development Indicators.

THE CHOICE

Should we enjoy life now, consuming more oil and accelerating the destruction of the ozone layer, or tip the world into a recession of unprecedented scale in order to reduce consumption and forestall other dire consequences? The ideal would be to find an intermediate option through the development of new energy technology that would be more efficient and less polluting: a means of maintaining economic growth without causing the ecological destruction of the planet. This is the great challenge to science and technology in the years to come.

But at the present, no such solution is in sight. Those technologies have not been sufficiently developed, so far.

Under these circumstances, the choice should be clear. The world will opt to go on as it always has done, without worrying much about what might happen in the future. Oil consumption will continue to rise, and pollution, global warming and the deterioration of the ozone layer will intensify, as well. For now, there is no way to promote economic growth without consuming more oil.

The threat now is not the big meteorites, UFOs, or even terrorists. The certain threat is a complete oil crisis, in the near future. The accelerated decline has been projected to begin after oil production worldwide reaches its maximum levels — and when half of the world's reserves are consumed. Some geologists estimated that that point would be reached in 2002, others estimate 2006, still others 2008. But all agree that it will happen in the first decade of the present century.

That does not mean that the world will be left entirely without oil from one day to another; but every day the supply will be tighter and the fight to get more will become all the sharper.

A VERIFIABLE HYPOTHESIS

The hypothesis that oil will run out soon, on a worldwide scale, can be proven. The oil reserves are declining in the country that was the leading producer and exporter until just a few years ago. The United States has gone from being the largest exporter to becoming the largest importer of crude oil. Prospectors are discovering just one barrel for every five produced, at the moment. And furthermore, many of the oil fields of the world are in decline, including the North Sea, in Mexico and in Venezuela.

Social science research is different from gelogy: there is less direct information, and much information that is generally not available at all, or is dispersed and is not organized in a way that is conducive to comparison and analysis. The work of researchers, then, consists in gathering information that both supports and contradicts the thesis, finding indirect ways to test it, and drawing up comparisons and interpretations. Applying the scientific method one may formulate a hypothesis of what might happen in the future — of course, with a high degree of uncertainty, because in social sciences none of the analytical methods are precise. The researcher may consider the big picture, identify trends, and analyze them, then scrutinize the past to infer something about the future. But there are situations in which mankind has no experience. For example, how can we anticipate what will happen when a fundamental resource like oil runs out entirely? That is a brand new experience. In the past, it was always possible to find a substitute for a commodity in short supply.

Perhaps the closest parallel in history is the experimentation of the National Socialist government in World War II that tried to replace gasoline with a synthetic fuel made from coal. They had some success but could not produce enough. Hitler could not replace oil. During World War II the governments of Germany, Italy and Japan were acutely conscious of the vulnerability posed by their lack of local energy sources. Historians show, for example, that Hitler's decision to invade the Soviet Union had among its fundamental strategic objectives to take possession of that country's petroleum resources, in the first instance, and from that strategic position to dominate the oil industry of the Middle East. Attacking the Soviet Union was clearly a highly risky venture that could only be undertaken if there was no alternative. Hitler must have had a compelling reason to do it. The Soviet Union's abundant oil would have constituted such a reason. Mussolini looked for the same thing in Africa: to get oil. Japan did the same in Asia. The 1991 Gulf War and the current US occupation of Iraq are, plausibly, further examples. As a whole, they show to what lengths man can go to increase his access to petroleum.

WE ALL LOVE A HAPPY ENDING

Humans feel a certain attraction to fantasy. The success of the mass media — cinema, theater, television, radio, magazines and newspapers — lies in the fact that each one presents and plays with fantasy to attract people. The reality, the truth, is usually very unpleasant and very powerful. Most people have little tolerance for it. Everybody has his own fantasy and is happy believing in it. Politicians of every stripe, democratic or authoritarian, and economists, those who believe in the free market as well as socialists, each person in his own way lives in his own illusion and tries to express it to others.

One of the common fantasies in the modern world — stimulated by many interested sectors — is the belief that earth's resources will last forever. It was only in the 1970s that a conservationist movement first arose that broke that illusion on a wide scale. Only then did an awareness begin to spread of the need to expend resources more responsibly.

Throughout history, man has appealed to myths to feed his fantasies. Arriving in America, Spanish settlers created the El Dorado Legend, according to which a region of South America gold supposedly lay ready for the taking, right on the Earth's surface. The idea of such a place was alluring enough to inspire them to cross the sea, climb mountains and trek through jungles, deep into the continent, from the Venezuela-Guayana region to the Inca Empire, in today's Peru. Gold fever also caught on among emigrants arriving in North America. The common element was the supposed existence of immense treasures. Oil has been called "black gold." There is no public discussion of how long the supply will hold out.

Most people, in most countries, take for granted that there is plenty of oil and therefore the topic does not generate any concern. But oil is already beginning to run out. That the Middle East (home to three-fourths of the proven oil reserves) has become a battleground where the most powerful nations skirmish shamelessly, pounding each other and everyone who gets in the way, reveals the ruthless conflict that must ensue when the word gets out that the oil is almost gone.

THE PRICE OF SCARCITY

Oil has never reached its appropriate price. That its supply is limited has never been factored into its value, because it has always seemed to be virtually infinite in supply. Still, the price of oil was raised by 3,200% between 1970 and 1980, from $1.25 dollars per barrel to $40 dollars, the highest it had ever been until then. This phenomenon might occur again and a clear example in this sense is the great jump in the oil prices in August 2005, when it surpassed the amount of $60 per barrel.

In the first year of oil exploitation, 1860, oil was quoted at $9.59 per barrel. The price stayed at an average of $6 up to 1873, when it stabilized at less than $2 and stayed there until 1973, that is to say, for 100 years, when oil rose far above the $2 mark. (See Chapter 14 for more details.)

In those hundred years between 1873 and 1973, extraordinary changes took place in the world; industrialization took off, technological breakthroughs were frequent and far-reaching, and wars of unprecedented scale mobilized huge fleets of motor-driven vehicles. However, none of that significantly altered the price of oil. How can it be explained, for example, that during World War I, the Great Depression, and the Spanish Civil War that was a prelude to World War II, oil remained steady at $2 dollars a barrel?

What happened in 1973 to break this stability? Understanding this process is very important to understanding what may occur in the future. If the price jumps 3,200% again between 2002 and 2012, the price will be $512 dollars per barrel.

It was a political decision of the Arab oil-producing countries that changed the price in 1973. And whether it comes as a "political decision" or "the invisible hand" of the "free market," such a shift may happen again, from one day to the next, when it can no longer be denied that oil reserves are not growing nearly fast enough to guarantee the future supply.

For now, tight oil production is explained away as a consequence of arcane economic and political decisions related to the low oil prices at the end of the 1990s, which discouraged new exploration and drilling. No one has acknowledged that production is down because oil is running out. Some oil-producing countries decided between 1999 and 2001 to do all they could to attain production reductions; it is possible that they were acting as a consequence of the awareness about the scarcity situation. If that is the case, then petroleum prices will remain high in the foreseeable future. What is more, OPEC countries might decide to cut production further, without openly stating that it is due to their conviction that oil is running out. They can cut production as they have done up to now without giving any explanations while, in reality, being keenly aware of the necessity of cutting back on production to make the remaining oil last longer.

CHAPTER 5. FINITE RESOURCES

Oil is just one example. The earth's other essential gifts like water and food are also being exhausted as a result of man's predatory action.

In the course of millennia, the plant and animal life on earth has evolved, with some new species appearing as others became extinct. By the 20th century, as a consequence of manmade environmental pressures, numerous species have gone from plentiful to the verge of extinction in a matter of years. One of the more symbolic cases worldwide is the panda bear of China, and the North American buffalo that once roamed the prairies.

EXTINCT SPECIES

By 2004, the official studies of the International Union for Conservation of Nature and Natural Resources noted that 237 wild species had disappeared in the United States since observers began taking note. The country with the second greatest number of missing species for 2004 was the French Polynesia, with 76 species reaching extinction. Mankind has sometimes claimed for himself a role as "steward of the earth." Any steward who lost this much of what was under his care would surely be fired, and it is not inconceivable that nature is about to get rid of this steward, as well.

Table 9. Animals Declared Extinct, 2004, by Country.

Country	Extinct Species
United States	237
French Polynesia	76
Tanzania	46
Uganda	46
Kenya	45
Mauritius	40
Australia	37
Saint Helena	29
Mexico	26
Sri Lanka	19
New Zealand	19
Japan	15
Cook Islands	15
Haiti	12
Norfolk Island	9
Martinique	8
Dominican Republic	8
Canada	7
Cuba	7
Guadeloupe	7

Source: International Union for Conservation of Nature and Natural Resources.
Red list of threatened species 2004. Table 6A.

Table 10. Animals Declared Extinct, 2004, by Continent.

Continent	Extinct Species
America	355
Africa	235
Oceania	177
Asia	121
Europe	22
Total World	910

Source: International Union for Conservation of Nature and Natural Resources.
Red list of threatened species 2004. Table 6A.

The International Union for Conservation of Nature and Natural Resources also provides numbers on species in danger of extinction. In 2004, the United States headed the list with a total of 903 species at risk, followed by Australia with 562.

Table 11. Threatened Species* (Animals), 2004, by Country.

Country	Threatened Species
United States	903
Australia	562
Mexico	487
Indonesia	450
Colombia	371
Ecuador	336
China	330
Brazil	316
India	306
South Africa	282
Madagascar	254
Philippines	244
Peru	234
Malaysia	209
Japan	193
Tanzania	177
New Guinea	153
Venezuela	152
Cameroon	150
Russia	144

* Critically endangered, endangered, vulnerable.
Source: International Union for Conservation of Nature and Natural Resources.
Red list of threatened species 2004. Table 6A.

Table 12. Threatened Species* (Animals), 2004, by Continent.

Continent	Threatened Species
America	4,790
Asia	4,103
Africa	2,831
Europe	1,759
Oceania	1,255
Total World	14,738

Source: International Union for Conservation of Nature and Natural Resources.
Red list of threatened species 2004. Table 6A.

ENDANGERED MAMMALS, 2002

Indonesia heads the list with 147 mammal species in danger of extinction, followed by India, 88, Brazil, 81, and China, 79.

Table 13. Mammal Species in Danger of Extinction, 2002, by Country.

Country	Total Species	Threatened Species	% of Total
Indonesia	515	147	28.54
India	390	88	22.56
Brazil	394	81	20.55
China	394	79	20.05
Mexico	491	70	14.25
Australia	252	63	25.00
Kenya	359	51	14.20
Madagascar	141	50	35.46
Philippines	153	50	32.67
Malaysia	300	50	16.66
Peru	460	49	10.65
Russia	269	45	16.72
Tanzania	316	42	13.29
South Africa	247	42	17.00
Vietnam	213	40	18.77
Colombia	359	41	11.42
United States	428	37	8.64
Japan	188	37	19.68
Argentina	320	34	10.62
Ecuador	302	33	10.92

Source: World Bank. World Development Indicators 2005. Table 3.4. Pages 142-144.

Brazil tops the list with 114 species of birds in danger of extinction for the year 2002.

Table 14. Bird Species in Danger of Extinction, 2002, by Country.

Country	Species in 2000	Threatened Species	% of the total
Brazil	686	114	16.61
Indonesia	929	114	12.27
Colombia	708	78	11.01
Peru	695	76	10.93
China	618	74	11.97
India	458	72	15.72
Philippines	404	67	16.58
New Zealand	-	63	
Ecuador	640	62	9.68
United States	508	55	10.82
Argentina	362	39	10.77
Mexica	440	39	8.86
Russia	528	38	7.19
Malaysia	254	37	14.56
Thailand	285	37	12.98
Australia	497	35	7.44
Vietnam	262	35	14.12
Japan	210	34	16.19
Tanzania	229	33	14.41
New Guinea	414	32	7.72

Source: World Bank. World Development Indicators 2005. Table 3.4. Pages 142-144.

ENDANGERED PLANT SPECIES

Malaysia had by far the greatest number of endangered plants in 2002, with Indonesia and Sri Lanka at half that.

Table 15. Plant Species in Danger of Extinction, 2002, by Country.

Country	Species in 2000	Threatened Species	% of Total
Malaysia	15,500	681	4.39
Indonesia	29,375	384	1.30
Sri Lanka	3,314	280	8.40
Peru	17,144	269	1.56
India	18,664	244	1.30
Tanzania	10,008	236	2.35
Jamaica	3,308	206	6.22
Panama	9,915	193	1.94
Ecuador	19,362	197	1.01
Philippines	8,931	193	2.16
China	32,200	168	0.52
Madagascar	9,505	162	1.70
Cuba	6,522	160	2.45
Cameroon	8,260	155	1.87
New Guinea	11,544	142	1.23
Nigeria	4,715	119	2.52
Ghana	3,725	115	3.06
Costa Rica	12,119	109	0.89
Honduras	5,680	108	1.90
Cote D'Ivoire	3,660	101	2.75

Source: World Bank. World Development Indicators 2005. Table 3.4

DEFORESTATION

Brazil leads the field, this time, with 22,264 square kilometers deforested between 1990 and 2000. In second place is Indonesia with 13,124 kilometers.

Table 16. Deforestation, 1990–2000, by Country.

Country	Km^2
Brazil	22,264
Indonesia	13,124
Sudan	9,589
Zambia	8,509
Mexico	6,306
Congo	5,324
Nigeria	3,984
Zimbabwe	3,199
Peru	2,688
Argentina	2,851
Malaysia	2,377
Cameroon	2,218
Venezuela	2,175
Colombia	1,905
Ecuador	1,372
Kenya	931
Philippines	887
Malawi	707
Nigeria	617
Panama	519

Source: World Bank. 2001 World Development Indicators. Pages 138-140.

According to the United Nations Report Geo2000, between 1980 and 1990 Latin America lost 5.5 million hectares of tropical forests, an amazing figure. Of the total deforestation worldwide, 25% of the destruction was in the tropical rain forest and 43% in subtropical forests. In Central America the dry forests were reduced drastically to only 4% of their original area; that is to say that 96% of its surface has been destroyed.

The Report reckons that in next few decades population growth, increased demand for firewood and the conversion of forests into agricultural lands will entail the destruction of still greater areas of the Latin American forests. And it stresses that the region suffers an imbalance in terms of reforestation; since 1981-1990 only 373,000 hectares were reforested; in other words, only 1/25 of the land is replanted. The Americas possess the greatest water reserves in the world, but one can deduce that this privileged situation will be affected by the destruction of the forests.

The World Bank considers that "nearly half of the world forests have been destroyed, most of them during the last forty years of the 20th century. Also, 40% of the Earth's surface is arid and vulnerable to degradation."[17]

The number of species existent on earth is considered to be between 10 and 100 million. Of them, only 1.7 million were identified and described by the end of the 20th entury. Fifty percent of those live in the tropical forests; therefore, the disappearance of the forests means the disappearance of many species that inhabits them. "If the deforestation continues at the present rate, between 2 and 8% of the earth's species will disappear in the first twenty five years of the 21st century."[18]

Pollution not only destroys habitats directly but appears to be creating changes in the world climate.

SOUTH AMERICA'S ELECTRIC POWER CRISIS

The destructive effects of deforestation in South America are of such magnitude that the river flow in the whole Amazon Region is diminishing drastically. Brazil, the country with the fifth-largest population, was the eighth economy of the world in 1999. As a consequence of the drought that affected the hydroelectric plants in June 2001, a severe program of energy rationing in the north and the center of that country was instigated; this included big cities like Brazilia and Rio de Janeiro. The rationing program limited production activities and especially industry. The government closed down night shows and turned off warning lights, restricted bank hours and commercial activities, generating unemployment and other social problems.

As of 2001, Brazil obtained 90% of its electricity from hydraulic sources. But the lingering drought created major difficulties. Forests affect the hydrological cycle; and deforestation has gone hand in hand with increasing droughts in the whole Amazon region, especially because of the voracious activity of the gold and diamond mining and timber companies that have devastated thousands of hectares of trees and altered the ecological balance of the region.

Brazil has recognized its vulnerability and it resolved in 2002 to build some 50 gas-based thermoelectric plants. That gas would be obtained from its

17. World Bank, Washington, Fifth Annual Conference on Environmental and Socially Sustainable Development, October 1997, page 117.
18. Ibid., page 229.

neighbor, Bolivia, which is significantly stepping up its gas production. Brazil also has planned to build a huge new dam in the Amazon, but that project is in jeopardy as the water sources in the region continue to deteriorate.

In Venezuela, the river that feeds one of the country's main hydroelectric dams, Guri Dam — near the Brazilian border — has been shrinking at an alarming rate. Caroni River is one of the largest in the world. From its origins at the frontier with Brazil till it joins the Orinoco River, it has a slope of more than 900 meters that gives it great potential to generate energy. The Guri Hydro-electric System generated more than 75% of the electric power of Venezuela in 2000 and it also supplied Brazil; for that very purpose a great transmission network was built at the end of 1990s. So when the Guri is affected, it not only hurts Venezuela but also northeastern Brazil.

The Venezuelan Ministry of Energy and Mines launched a media campaign to promote electricity conservation in industry and at home. The Ministry's goal[19] was to reduce a total of 9,000 gigawats in 2002, that is to say, 10.9% of the total capacity of electric generation. This came as a terrific shock; Venezuela had always enjoyed tremendous hydraulic resources. Venezuela had a capacity to generate of 82,562 gigawats an hour in 2000[20]; 76% of that total is produced through hydraulic sources.[21] Venezuela and Brazil will have to turn to thermo-electric generation to satisfy their future needs; that will mean major infra-structure costs for countries that are already burdened with gigantic foreign debts.

Generating electricity is a challenge for other countries in South America as well. Argentina contemplated an energy restriction in 2002; Chile already had similar problems in 1998, also as a consequence of a lingering drought.

What happened in South America is representative of what could happen in other regions of the world. The United States suffered its first major electric power generation crisis in California in 1999.

AS OIL USE DECREASES, NUCLEAR ENERGY USE INCREASES

Statistics on electricity generation show that gas and nuclear energy are being used more frequently as sources for generating electricity; it doubled between 1980 and 1997, according to studies carried out by the World Bank. Gas went from 8.8% in 1980 at 15.5% in 1997, while nuclear energy was increased from 8.7% to 17.3% in the same period. Coal also went up in that period from 33.1% to 38.4%.

---

19. *Diario El Nacional*. Caracas, Venezuela. November 16, 2001, page E6.
20. CVG. *Electrificación del Caroní*. Figures year 2000, page 34.
21. Ibid.

Conversely, hydroelectric generation was less worldwide, going from 20.4% to 18.2% in the period mentioned. The world is replacing the cleanest, least polluting sources for generating electricity with more polluting sources.

The use of oil in power generation dropped more sharply, falling by two-thirds from 28.5% in 1980 to only 9.1% in 1997. This reflects the efforts that were being made to reduce dependence on oil.

Table 17. Sources of Electricity, Percentage of Total Production. 1980-1997.

Trillion KWH		Hydro-electricity		Coal		Oil		Gas		Nuclear Energy		Other Sources*	
1980	1997	1980	1997	1980	1997	1980	1997	1980	1997	1980	1997	1980	1997
8,192.7	13,872.6	20.4	18.2	33.1	38.4	28.5	9.1	8.8	15.5	8.7	17.3	0.5	1.5

Source: The World Bank. 2000 World Development Indicators.
*geothermal, solar, eolic, etc.

In general, these figures show that while less oil is being used to generate electricity, its place has been taken by a perilous resource like nuclear energy. Some countries, like France and Germany, tripled their use of nuclear energy for power generation between 1980 and 1997. Belgium, Korea and Japan also dramatically increased their reliance on nuclear energy.

China has increased its use of coal. Coal is one of the biggest contributors of pollutants implicated in the greenhouse effect. Given the magnitude of China's population and its economy, any change in how China uses natural resources has an effect on the whole world.

Table 18. Sources of Electricity, Share of Total Production.
1980-1997.

Countries	Trillion KWH		Hydro-elec-tricity		Coal		Oil		Gas		Nuclear Energy		Other Sources	
	1980	1997	1980	1997	1980	1997	1980	1997	1980	1997	1980	1997	1980	1997
Argentina	40	72	38.1	39.1	2.5	1.0	31.9	3.6	21.0	44.9	5.9	11.0	0.6	0.4
Belgium	53	78	0.5	0.4	29.4	20.9	34.7	1.8	11.2	14.8	23.6	60.7	0.6	1.4
Brazil	139	307	92.5	90.8	2.0	1.8	3.8	3.2	—	0.4	—	1.0	1.7	2.8
China	313	1,163	18.6	16.8	57.0	74.2	24.2	7.2	0.2	0.6	—	1.2	—	—
Finland	41	69	25.1	17.7	42.6	28.3	10.8	2.0	4.2	10.0	17.2	30.2	0.1	11.8
France	257	499	26.9	12.5	27.2	5.2	18.9	1.5	2.7	1.0	23.8	79.3	0.5	0.5
Germany	466	548	4.1	3.2	62.9	53.4	5.7	1.3	14.2	9.2	11.9	31.1	1.2	1.8
Japan	573	1,300	15.4	8.7	9.6	19.1	46.2	18.2	14.2	20.5	14.4	31.0	0.2	2.5
Korea	37	244	5.3	1.2	6.7	37.4	78.7	16.8	—	13.0	9.3	31.6	—	—
Mexico	67	175	25.2	15.1	—	10.0	57.9	54.3	15.5	11.5	—	6.0	1.4	3.1
Russia	805	833	16.1	18.8	—	16.8	77.2	5.3	—	45.3	6.7	13.1	—	0.7
Ukraine	236	178	5.7	5.5	—	27.6	88.3	4.3	—	17.9	6.0	44.7	—	—
UK	284	344	1.4	1.2	73.2	34.8	11.7	2.3	0.7	31.3	13.0	28.5	—	1.9
US	2,427	3,671	11.5	9.0	51.2	53.8	10.8	2.9	15.3	13.8	11.0	18.2	0.2	2.3
Venezuela	37	75	39.6	76.3	—	—	2.9	2.7	45.9	21.0	—	—	11.6	—

Source: The World Bank. 2000 World Development Indicators. Pages 146-149.
Other Sources: geothermal, sun, eolic, etc.

POPULATION AND FOOD, WATER AND ENERGY PRODUCTION

There are three legs that human life stands on, but with every passing year each of the three elements are scarcer. In the decades since 1970, the production of food worldwide grew at a moderate rate but the world population has grown dramatically.

Table 19. Population per Continent, in Millions.

	1950	1960	1970	1980	1985	1990	1995	1996
Total World	2,524	3,027	3,702	4,447	4,847	5,282	5,687	5,768
Africa	224	282	364	476	548	629	719	739
North America	172	204	232	255	268	282	297	299
Latin America	166	217	2,844	359	398	438	477	484
Asia	1,402	1,702	2,147	2,641	2,902	3,184	3,438	3,488
Europe	547	605	656	693	707	722	728	729
Oceania	13	16	19	23	25	26	28	29

Source: United Nations. Statistical Yearbook, 43rd issue. New York, 1999.

In 1950, the world population reached 2.524 billion people. Fifty-five years later, in 2005, the population expanded to 6.5 billion people. At that rate of expansion, by 2044 the Earth will have 13 billion inhabitants.

Between 1990 and 1997, the world population grew at an average of 1.47%. The production of cereals increased by 1.13%, meat production by 3.11% and milk by 0.11%. This means that the production of two categories of fundamental foods grew more slowly than the population grew.

If we add to the problem of scarce production the unjust distribution of food around the world, the future outlook is grave. It would take a massive change in agriculture politics as well as important technological breakthroughs that would make higher yields possible while simultaneously reducing environmental degradation to turn around this dire situation.

In the 1980s, the situation was different. Cereals production went up by 2.32% and meat production by 2.86%, a figure that exceeded the population growth of 1.76%. Milk production did not keep pace with the population growth even then.

Table 20. Food Production Worldwide, 1990s, in Millions of Metric Tons.

Years	Population	% Growth	Cereals MMT	% Growth	Meat MMT	% Growth	Milk MMT	% Growth
1990	5,282		1,950		178		544	
1991	5,350	1.29	1,882	-3.47	182	2.09	536	-1.47
1992	5,479	2.41	1,968	4.53	185	1.84	528	-1.38
1993	5,544	1.19	1,897	-3.58	191	2.83	528	-0.02
1994	5,630	1.55	1,955	3.03	199	4.39	532	0.64
1995	5,716	1.53	1,902	-2.71	209	4.93	538	1.25
1996	5,768	0.91	2,072	8.98	218	4.15	540	0.37
1997	5,849	1.40	2,096	1.16	221	1.58	548	1.39
Average Growth		1.47		1.13		3.11		0.11

Source: FAO Production Yearbook 1995, 1997. United Nations Demographic Yearbook 1992, 1993, 1994, 1995, 1996, 1997.

Table 21. Food Production Worldwide, 1980s, in Millions of Metric Tons.

Years	Population	% Growth	Cereals MMT	% Growth	Meat MMT	% Growth	Milk MMT	% Growth
1980	4,447		1,568		132		468	
1981	4,513	1.48	1,653	5.40	135	1.97	470	0.43
1982	4,590	1.71	1,703	3.06	136	1.07	481	2.38
1983	4,669	1.72	1,644	-3.49	141	3.13	500	3.85
1984	4,764	2.03	1,804	9.73	144	2.40	501	0.20
1985	4,836	1.51	1,840	1.98	152	5.33	509	1.73
1986	4,915	1.63	1,851	0.62	156	2.90	518	1.75
1987	4,996	1.65	1,789	-3.33	161	3.14	516	-0.38
1988	5,114	2.36	1,742	-2.65	168	4.38	524	1.43
1989	5,205	1.78	1,881	7.98	171	1.77	529	1.09
1990	5,295	1.73	1,955	3.92	175	2.53	533	0.63
Average Growth		1.76		2.32		2.86		1.31

Source: FAO Production Yearbook 1995, 1997. United Nations Demographic Yearbook 1992, 1993, 1994, 1995, 1996, 1997.

In the 1970s, the production of cereals went up slightly faster than the population. Meat production grew at 3.11% and milk production, 1.74%. In relative terms, we could consider this decade a good one in terms of food production.

Table 22. Food Production Worldwide, 1970s, in Millions of Metric Tons.

Years	Population	% Growth	Cereals MMT	% Growth	Meat MMT	% Growth	Milk MMT	% Growth
1970	3,617		1,214		105		396	
1971	3,688	1.96	1,316	8.46	108	3.15	399	0.78
1972	3,760	1.95	1,280	-2.80	110	2.01	408	2.32
1973	3,834	1.97	1,377	7.63	111	0.73	414	1.50
1974	3,892	1.51	1,335	-3.06	117	5.09	423	2.00
1975	3,951	1.52	1,379	3.30	123	5.00	430	1.72
1976	4,026	1.97	1,488	7.91	126	3.02	439	2.07
1977	4,103	1.91	1,478	-0.69	131	3.71	451	2.85
1978	4,258	3.78	1,598	8.16	135	2.89	458	1.57
1979	4,335	1.81	1,556	-2.63	139	3.21	464	1.17
1980	4,437	2.35	1,571	0.92	142	2.26	470	1.41
Average Growth		2.07		2.72		3.11		1.74

Source: FAO Production Yearbook 1995, 1997. United Nations Demographic Yearbook 1992, 1993, 1994, 1995, 1996, 1997.

POLLUTION DAMPENS FOOD PRODUCTION WORLDWIDE

If we compare the evolution of food production worldwide in recent decades we can see that there is a clear tendency toward diminished supplies relative to population.

The statistics show that the increase in production of food took an abrupt fall in the 1990s. That slowdown in growth has been attributed to the environmental damages wrought by the deterioration of the ozone layer and global warming. Meat production also grew at a lower rate in the 1970s to the 1980s; there was a recovery in the 1990s. The growth of milk production worldwide also dropped, from 1.74% in the 1970s to 0.11% in the 1990s.

This comparison demonstrates that worldwide we face a diminishing ability to increase production of critical food categories. The consequences are obvious.

Table 23. Average Growth of Population and of Food Production.

Decades	Population	Cereals	Meat	Milk
1990-1997	1.47	1.13	3.11	0.11
1980-1990	1.76	2.32	2.86	1.31
1970-1980	2.07	2.72	3.11	1.74

Sources: FAO Production Yearbook: 1970, 1971, 1972, 1973, 1975, 1979, 1980, 1981, 1982, 1983, 1984, 1985, 1986, 1987, 1988, 1989, 1990, 1995, 1997.
United Nations Demographic Yearbook 1992, 1993, 1994, 1995, 1996, 1997.

HUNGRY PEOPLE

According to the FAO (Food & Agriculture Organization of the UN), 25% of the world population's suffered malnutrition between 1969 and 1971. For the period 1979-1981, the figure decreased to 20%, that is to say, to 906 million people, and between 1988 and 1990 it was 16%, in other words 841 million people. This is a positive and hopeful trend. But this trend could be threatened if the worldwide production of food is for any reason restricted. If environmental conditions continue to deteriorate, the production of food could stop increasing altogether and may even begin to fall.

Table 24. Malnutrition in the World (per millions of people).

Year	World Population	People in Hunger	%
1970	3,697	918	24.8
1980	4,447	906	20.4
1990	5,285	841	15.9

Source: FAO — OMS 1992.

NOT A DROP TO DRINK

The water supply is also jeopardized by man's predatory attitude. The contamination of the rivers has reached alarming heights, as illustrated in United Nations figures published in the Statistical Yearbook 1993 about the overall quality of water in a group of rivers around the world.

India, one of the most populous countries in the world and, consequently, with a great need of water, had in those years the greatest number of rivers contaminated by fecal material. The Sabarmati River in Ahmedabad boasted the highest rate of fecal pollution in the world between 1984 and 1988: 1,724,783 coliforms for 100 milliliters. In contrast, we could mention the Mackenzie River in Canada, which between 1988 and 1992 presented levels of pollution of only 0.01 for 100 milliliters.

Equally alarming cases are present in Latin America. In Mexico, between 1987 and 1991, the Atoyac River registered a level of fecal pollution of 903,658 coliforms for 100 milliliters and many other rivers in that country had the same problem. In Brazil, the Paraiba do Sul River registered 24,239 fecal materials per 100 ml between 1984 and 1988. The Rio de la Plata in Argentina had a level of fecal contamination of 1,831 per 100 milliliters between 1987 and 1991.

Table 25. Water Quality (in fecal coliforms).

Country	River	Period	Coliforms per 100 ml.
Canada	Churchill River	1988-1992	0.01
Mexico	River Lerma	1985-1989	309,158
	River Atoyac	1987-1991	903,658
Argentina	Río de la Plata	1987-1991	1,831
Brazil	Rio Paraiba do Sul	1984-1988	24,239
Chile	Río Maipo	1984-1988	722
China	Yellow River	1987-1991	5,269
India	River Sabarmati	1984-1988	1,724,783
	River Narmada	1984-1988	630,430
Indonesia	Sunter River	1988-1992	689,468
	River Banjir Kana	1988-1992	785,681
Japan	Sagami River	1988-1992	6,724
Turquía	Sakaraya River	1984-1988	39,960
Belgium	Lys River	1987-1991	120,991
Holland	Rhine River.	1984-1988	52,877

Source: United Nations Statistical Yearbook. Thirty ninth issue 1994. Page 85.

But other polluting elements are also causing serious damage to the world's rivers. One United Nations study asserts that of eight major rivers in Brazil, six present high indexes of mercury contamination. The regional rivers, especially in Brazil and Venezuela, are seriously threatened by the deforestation of their sources and the use of mercury by miners. If the deterioration continues, in a few years the Amazon — that is the biggest forest reserve that is still left in the world — will have become a desert.

In 1998, China had the worst record in water emissions of organic pollutants, 8,491,856 kilograms a day, followed by the United States with 2,577,002 kilograms per day, India with 1,760,353 kilograms/day, Russia with 1,531,501, Japan with 1,391,281 kilograms/day and Brazil with 690,876 kilograms/day.

Table 26. Water Pollution (in kilograms per day).

Country	1980	1998
China	3,377,105	8,491,856
United States	2,742,993	2,577,002
India	1,422,564	1,760,353
Russia	—	1,531,501
Japan	1,456,016	1,391,281
Germany	—	811,316
United Kingdom	964,510	611,743
Brazil	866,790	690,876
France	729,776	585,382
Ukraine	—	518,996
Poland	580,869	386,376
Italy	442,712	359,578
Thailand	213,271	355,819
Spain	376,253	348,262
Indonesia	214,010	347,083
Rumania	343,315	333,168
Korea	281,900	317,903
South Africa	237,599	241,922
Egypt	169,146	225,843

Source: World Bank. 2001 World Development Indicators. Pages 146-149.

POPULATION DISTRIBUTION

About 60% of the world population lives in Asia, 12% in Africa, 12.63% in Europe, 8% in Latin America; and 5% in North America. Oceania comprises just 0.49% of world population. The world's wealth is distributed in quite a different proportion, whether we speak of natural resources or capital. The relationship is rather an inverse one.

Table 27. Population Distribution. 1996.

Regions	Millions of People	% of World Population
Africa	739	12.8
North America	299	5.2
Latin America	484	8.4
Asia	3,488	60.5
East Asia	1,434	24.9
South Central Asia	1,392	24.1
South East Asia	490	8.5
Western Asia	182	3.2
Europe	729	12.6
Eastern Europe	310	5.4
Northern Europe	93	1.6
Southern Europe	144	2.5
Western Europe	182	3.2
Oceania	29	0.5
Total World	5,768	100.0

Source: United Nations Statistical Yearbook, Forty Third Issue. New York 1999.

WATER

The need for water is even more fundamental than the need for oil, and its shortage is perhaps more apparent, albeit often dismissed as merely a seasonal, regional or cyclical problem. There have always been regions where the availability of water has been poor and others where it has been plentiful; but in recent years, due to over-use of the underground aquifers and due to pollution of sources that once were pristine, even areas where traditionally water has been abundant now experience shortages.

Table 28. Available Water by Region:

Regions	Annual Internal Renewable Water Resources		Percentage of Population Living in Countries with Scarce Annual Per Capita Resources	
	Total	Per Capita	less than 1000 m^3	1000 to 2000 m^3
	thousands km^2	thousands of m^3		
Sub-Saharan Africa	3.8	7.1	8	16
East Asia and Pacific	9.3	5.3	<1	6
Middle Asia	4.9	4.2	0	0
Eastern Europe and Former USSR	4.7	11.4	3	19
Western Europe	2.0	4.6	6	15
Middle East and North of Africa	0.3	1.0	53	18
Latin America and the Caribbean	10.6	23.9	<1	4
Canada and US	5.4	19.4	0	0
Total World	40.9	7.7	4	8

Source: World Bank. World Development Report 1992. Development and Environment. Page 48.

DRYING UP IN THE MIDDLE EAST

The Middle East and North Africa have long been arid regions. In some parts, with less than one cubic meter of water annually per inhabitant, are too dry to support human survival. For a simple comparison, as Table 28 shows, water availability — renewable domestic water resources — in the United States and Canada amounts to 19.4 annual cubic meters for person that means 18 times more than the availability for people in the Middle East and North Africa.

As a United Nations report on world hunger once noted, "a hungry man is an angry man." A thirsty man is, too. The difficulty of obtaining water and food has not helped calm things down in Africa and the Middle East, where there is little to go around and many mouths to feed.

As evidence of the water crisis in the Middle East and in North of Africa, we can look again at the status of the major rivers. The Nile River, which has been a vital source of water since civilization began, has begun to be reduced in size so that every day the amount of water that it discharges into the Mediterranean Sea decreases. The Jordan River has also been shrinking and this only intensifies the conflict between Arabs and Jews. The rivers Tigris and Euphrates are also in danger.

A population that does not have enough water or food may find no other alternative than to fight each other for the little that does exist. Beyond ideological or religious differences, at bottom the Middle East crisis can be seen in the light of competition for vital natural resources.

The Sahara Desert is inexorably expanding, forcing the North Africa population to emigrate — mostly toward Europe, which creates other sorts of problems.

On October 26, 2005, an invasion of African citizens sought to enter Europe. The Spanish cities of Ceuta and Melilla in the north of Africa received the pressure of hundreds of immigrants that assaulted the fence officially dividing them from Morocco. Eleven people were killed and dozens wounded. Desperate attempts to flee the continent can only escalate if the rest of the world does not adopt economic and social policies to help the African countries. The immigrants leave their countries because of the critical lack of water, food, and employment. And this is just the beginning.

WATER SHORTAGE IN ASIA

In Asia as well, the mightiest rivers are in a state of decline. The flow of the Yangtze River, the largest in China, is affected by the construction of dams for power generation. The Yellow River is progressively drying up and the same phenomenon can be seen with the major rivers of India.

A March 2005 report by the World Wildlife Fund, WWF, reveals that the glaciers of the Himalaya are receding by 10 to 15 meters a year, and that average is increasing due to global warming. The Gangotri glacier in India is receding by 23 meters per year. The glaciers of the Himalaya feed seven of the biggest rivers in Asia: the Ganges, Indus, Brahmaputra, Thanlwin, Mekong, Yangtze and the Yellow River; and in the process they support the lives of hundreds of millions of people in China, India and Nepal. Thawing, the glaciers can cause floods; that will necessarily be followed by a reduced availability of water.

EVEN AMERICA IS GOING DRY

The Americas had the most extensive renewable water resources, conferring on them a special privilege. However, in spite of that abundance some regions already are feeling the pinch. Caracas, the capital of Venezuela, had water rationing for the whole of 2000 and 2001. The shortage also affected other nations. In the 1992 World Development Report[22] the World Bank highlights

22. Page 51

"situations of lack in certain water basins in the north of China, the west and south of India and Mexico."

Much water is wasted through carelessness on a grand scale, and growing contamination contributes to making a critical situation in many countries that had abundant reserves. Even a renewable resource like this, so often taken for granted, can be depleted if we do not use it rationally.

In North America, the Colorado River has been an important source of water to seven western states: Colorado, Utah, New Mexico, Wyoming, California, Arizona and Nevada; but in recent years the river's flow has been reduced so much that it no longer reaches the Pacific Ocean — neither in summer nor in winter. The river is slowly drying up, due to the intense use in irrigation and industrial and residential uses. This phenomenon, in turn, affects other rivers and the problem of water shortages is every day more critical.

According to the US Census Bureau in 2002 the United States had 281,421,906 inhabitants. The seven states in the Southwest represent 14% of the states and they harbor at least 50 million people. (In 2002, Colorado had a population of 4.3 million people, Utah 2.2 million, New Mexico 1.8 million, Wyoming 0.49 million, California 33.8 million, Arizona 5.1 million and Nevada 1.9. This means that at least 18% of the population of the United States already has a potential problem of water supply.) A report of the US Department of the Interior on May 3, 2004, said that if the trend continues, by 2006 or 2007 a water emergency might be declared. Yet the demand on the waters of the Colorado River continue to increase due to the population's increase, the growing needs of agriculture and other production activities.

The conflicts among the states that share the waters of the Colorado River are growing, too. Colorado, Utah, Wyoming and New Mexico have demanded that the Secretary of the Interior implement conservation and allocation measures that have been rejected by the other states.

EUROPE

Table 28 shows that Europe enjoys a water capacity of 4,600 cubic meters per capita, for 12.6% of the world population in 1996.

ASIA

Asia and the Pacific region had an annual water capacity of 5.3 cubic meters per capita. Southern Asia had 4.2 cubic meters for person. Asia, the most populous continent, had annual water resources of 9.5 (5.3+4.2) cubic meters per capita, that is to say, half that of Canada and the United States.

MIDDLE EAST

The Middle East has more oil but less water and food; North America has abundant water and food but needs oil. This sets up a certain geostrategic dynamic that is rife with tension.

Asia has neither food nor oil sufficient to lift its half of the world population to the living standard enjoyed in the West; Africa is even worse off, yet it has the highest birth rate (41% between 1990 and 1995).

Table 29. World Demographic Trends and Population Density.

Continents	Annual birthrate (per thousands)	Annual mortality (per thousands)	Surface (thousands of Kms$^{2)}$	Density *
	1990-1995	1990-1995	1996	1996
Africa	41	14	30,306	24
Asia	24	8	31,764	110
Eastern Europe	12	11	22,968	32
Western Europe	11	10	1,107	164
Latin America	25	7	20,533	24
North America	15	9	21,517	14
Oceania	19	8	8,537	3

Population per square kilometer of surface area. Source: United Nations Statistical Yearbook, Forty third Issue, New York 1999. Page 12.Data available as 30 September 1998.

North America and Europe will continue to exert the greatest pressure on Earth's resources. And this has complex political, economical and military implications. Just check the world oil-demand projections to 2020 as estimated by the United States International Agency of Energy.[23]

There is no permanent state of equilibrium or of dominance. Equilibrium and dominance are only temporary and relative. Only change is permanent. At certain moments of history, specific regions and countries acquired control of most of the resources and dominated the rest of the world. But it is a dynamic process that constantly changes and tends to become contrary. Since the 15th century the European powers — especially England, Spain, France and Portugal — controlled the world and secured access to the most natural wealth as consequence of conquering the Americas and dominating Asia and Africa. But that situation was transformed over time and the center of world power shifted from Europe to the United States and the Soviet Union, since at least the second half of the 20th

---

23. Energy Information Administration International Energy Outlook 2000, page 170.

century. Having control over natural resources is synonymous with material power. Natural resources constitute the axis, the base upon which political and economic relationships are sustained. The battle for economic dominance is fundamentally a battle for the possession and control over natural resources. Science and technology alone are not enough. Science and technology need raw material, need the earth's resources to achieve their objectives. All of economic development is built upon two fundamental criteria: the availability of resources and man's creative capacity to transform those resources.

HISTORICAL EVIDENCE, THE EXAMPLE OF THE POTOSÍ MINES

Deposits of natural resources have been depleted in many parts of the world. For example, one of the biggest silver reserves in the world was mined out: the Potosí Mines, in what is now Bolivia; the mines were discovered between 1545 and 1548. This region was one of the world's most prosperous at that time due to the silver exploitation. Historians confirm that at the peak of production, the Potosí region was the center of Latin American colonial life. At the beginning of the 17th century, Potosí City had thirty-six splendidly ornamented churches, thirty-six casinos and fourteen dance saloons. In 1579, there were already 800 professional gamblers and 120 celebrated prostitutes in whose radiant salons those who had made their fortunes through mining congregated. Between 1503 and 1560, 185,000 kilos of gold and 16 million kilos of silver arrived in Spain's San Lucar de Barrameda port. In little more than a century, the silver transported to Spain exceeded the total of European holdings by three times. The metals that so lofted the aspirations of the new colonial domains stimulated, indeed, made possible, European economic development.[24] But what goes up must come down; it lasted only until the 17th century — and today Bolivia's Potosí region is one of the poorest in the world. Potosí City is a city of ruins.

MINAS GERAIS'S GOLD

Similarly, the Minas Gerais region in Brazil was rich in gold and diamonds in the mid-18th century; only memories remain. In that century, Brazilian gold production surpassed the total volume of gold that Spain had extracted from its colonies in the two previous centuries. At the time of the discovery, Salvador de Bahía, in the north, was the capital of Brazil; the agricultural economy (dominated by forest production and sugar production) had been most important until then. That changed when gold mining began in earnest. The big mines were located in the south. The political and economic center moved there, and since

---

24. *Las Venas Abiertas de América Latina.* Galeano, Eduardo. Editorial Siglo XXI, Mexico 1971, pages 33-35.

1763 Rio de Janeiro was the Brazilian capital. As a consequence of the mining expansion, new cities arose. Ouro Preto's Villa Rica, created in 1761, became the center of gold exploitation in Brazil. It ended up as one of the continent's most prosperous cities. Ouro Preto was called the "Potosí of Gold." This town had all the Europe and Asian luxuries. But the wealth disappeared when the gold ran out, and it became one of the poorest regions in Brazil.[25]

THE GOLD OF PERU AND THE SILVER OF MEXICO

And there are other examples in Latin America: the lost gold mines of Peru, founded by Francisco Pizarro, and the silver mines of Zacatecas and Guanajuato, opened in 1700 in Mexico. In Venezuela, mining created a new economy in some regions but also new miseries. The rich Guayana (Amazonia) Region has largely been denuded by miners, destroying large parts of the most important forest and biological reserve in this half of the world. Rubber, too, was also abundant in South America; now it is practically nonexist because of the intense exploitation that was practiced, especially in Brazil and in the south of Venezuela.

OIL IS NOT AN EXCEPTION

Some countries have already noticed that oil is running out. For example Ecuador, which had some success in oil exploration in the last several decades, confirmed that their reserves were limited and accordingly they limited their production. This forced the country to quit OPEC, after having invested great efforts in order to join it. The same thing has happened with other producers, such as Gabon, who joined OPEC only to leave it soon after.

Venezuela suffered an important reduction in its reserves of light oil in the 1980s, but its total reserves did not diminish because starting in 1986, part of the heavy oil reserves in the Orinoco Belt were registered as proven reserves. Likewise, Mexico categorized its reserves of gas together with the proven petroleum reserves in the 1980s. This explains how Venezuela and Mexico boosted their apparent share of world reserves in the 1980s.

REFLECTION ON GROWTH

Consumption increases in step with the growth of the world economy. But all growth has an end. Economic cycles are a good example. Moments of great expansion and recession are generally moments when we exert greater or less pressure on our resources. Most of the economic growth and the major scientific

---

25. Ibid., pages 77-78.

and technological advances reached in the 20th century relied on one thing: the intensive use of petroleum as an energy source. There is no economic growth without a more intense use of energy and, in the modern world, energy is synonymous with petroleum. But the use of energy has a high price: the pollution and destruction of the planet. Man is the only species known to destroy its own habitat. Wild animals do not destroy their nests or their breeding grounds, nor the area where they live and hunt. Man does.

The fundamental concept that can be derived from all the foregoing and from the statistics that will be presented below is that, on a massive and global scale, man is in the process of using up a wide range of natural resources that are critical to his own well-being and even survival. The dawning recognition of this situation has already begun to show consequences.

In the next chapter we will take a look at the major petroleum countries for the year 2000 and then we will analyze in detail the projected demand, production, reserves and consumption rates.

CHAPTER 6. REALITY 2000

The members of the Organization of Petroleum Exporting Countries, OPEC, contributed 42.1% of the world oil production for the year 2000. The biggest that year was Saudi Arabia, with 8,094,000 barrels/day. Russia, not an OPEC member, was in second place, with 7,459,000 barrels/day. The US (also non-OPEC) was third, with 5,821,000 barrels/day. Together, these three countries accounted for almost a third of world production.

Table 30. Main Oil-Producing Countries. 2000.

Countries	Production (thousands of barrels/day)	% of Total World Production
Saudi Arabia *	8,094	12.3
Russia and Former USSR	7,459	11.3
United States	5,821	8.8
Iran *	3,661	5.6
China	3,228	4.9
Norway	3,182	4.8
Mexico	3,012	4.6
Venezuela *	2,891	4.4
Iraq *	2,810	4.3
United Kingdom	2,378	3.6
United Arab Emirates *	2,174	3.3
Nigeria *	2,053	3.1
Kuwait *	1,996	3.0
Canada	1,411	2.1
Libya *	1,347	2.0
Indonesia *	1,272	1.9
Brazil	1,233	1.9
Oman	898	1.4
Algeria *	796	1.2
Argentina	780	1.2
Angola	745	1.1
Colombia	686	1.0
Qatar *	648	1.0
India	645	1.0
Malaysia	599	0.9
Total for these countries	58,819	90.9
Total world	65,825	100.0

OPEC. Annual Statistical Bulletin 2000. * Countries members of the OPEC.

OPEC

Of the total production worldwide (65.8 million barrels/day in 2000), OPEC countries contributed 42.1%.

Table 31. Production: OPEC versus Non-OPEC. 2000.

OPEC		Non-OPEC		
thousands of barrels/day	*%*	*thousands of barrels/day*	*%*	*Total*
27,742	42.1	38,083	57.9	65,825

Source: OPEC Annual Statistical Bulletin 2000.

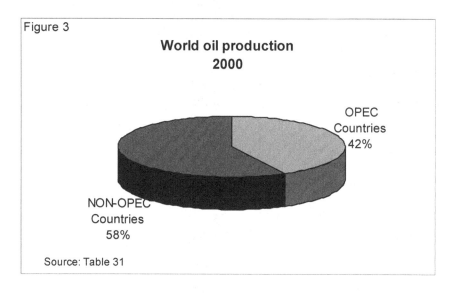

Figure 3

World oil production 2000

OPEC Countries 42%

NON-OPEC Countries 58%

Source: Table 31

Arabia also has the most oil reserves, 24.39% as of 2000. Iraq had the second most that year, 10.44%. The OPEC countries together hold 78.5% of the world's reserves.

Table 32. Proven Oil Reserves, by Country. 2000.

Country	Millions of Barrels	% of Total
Saudi Arabia *	262,766	24.39
Iraq *	112,500	10.44
Iran *	99,530	9.24
United Arab Emirates *	97,800	9.08
Kuwait *	96,500	8.96
Venezuela *	76,848	7.13
Russia and Former USSR	65,305	6.06
Libya *	36,000	3.34
Nigeria *	34,458	3.20
Mexico	28,260	2.62
China	24,000	2.23
United States	21,765	2.02
Norway	13,158	1.22
Qatar *	13,157	1.22
Algeria *	11,314	1.05
Canada	8,726	0.81
Brazil	8,100	0.75
Oman	5,700	0.53
Angola	5,412	0.50
Indonesia *	5,122	0.48
United Kingdom	5,002	0.46
Malaysia	3,900	0.36
Argentina	3,071	0.29
Ecuador	3,040	0.28
Australia	2,895	0.27
Colombia	2,577	0.24
Total, these countries	1,046,906	97.16
Total world reserves	1,077,500	100.00

*OPEC members. Source: Annual Statistical Bulletin 2000.

OPEC RESERVES

The total reserves worldwide were 1,077,500 million barrels in 2000; the OPEC countries held 845,995 million of them, that is, 78.5% of the total.

Table 33. Oil Reserves, OPEC vs. Non-OPEC, 2000. Millions of barrels.

Total World	OPEC Countries	%	Non-OPEC Countries	%
1,077,500	845,995	78.5	231,505	21.5

Source: OPEC. Annual Statistical Bulletin 2000.

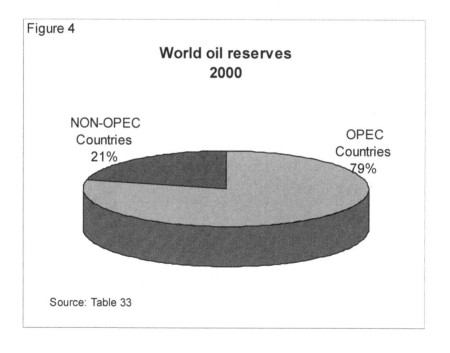

Figure 4

World oil reserves 2000

NON-OPEC Countries 21%

OPEC Countries 79%

Source: Table 33

OIL CONSUMERS

The United States, Japan and China are the greatest consumers of oil, accounting for 40% of the market for 2000. Russia and Germany come next.

Table 34. Oil Consumption. Top 20 Countries. 2000.

Country	Thousands of barrels/day	% of Total World Consumption
United States	18,650	26.42
Japan	5,287	7.49
China	4,675	6.62
Russia	3,765	5.33
Germany	2,689	3.81
India	2,080	2.95
Mexico	2,067	2.93
South Korea	2,022	2.86
Canada	2,003	2.84
France	1,994	2.82
Brazil	1,883	2.67
Italy	1,775	2.51
United Kingdom	1,667	2.36
Spain	1,289	1.83
Iran *	1,189	1.68
Saudi Arabia *	937	1.33
Australia	829	1.17
Thailand	663	0.94
Venezuela *	495	0.70
Holland	471	0.67
Total for these top 20	53,430	79.94
Total World Consumption	70,595	100.00

* OPEC members. Source: Annual Statistical Bulletin 2000.

CHAPTER 7. FORECASTING THE WORLD'S DEMAND FOR OIL

DEMAND WILL OUTSTRIP SUPPLY

The United States Department of Energy in its 2000 annual report projected that world oil consumption will jump from 73 million barrels/day in year 1997 to 112 million barrels/day in 2020. This represents an increase of 53%. This is an astronomical figure of with implications that are unimaginable at the present time, implications not only from the point of view of production but also for the environment, since current consumption levels are already bringing on a severe crisis.

Table 35. Projected Oil Consumption, 1990-2020. World. Millions of barrels/day.

History			Projections				Average
1990	1996	1997	2005	2010	2015	2020	
66.0	71.3	73.0	83.9	93.5	103.4	112.8	1.9

Source: Energy Information Administration. International Energy Outlook 2000.

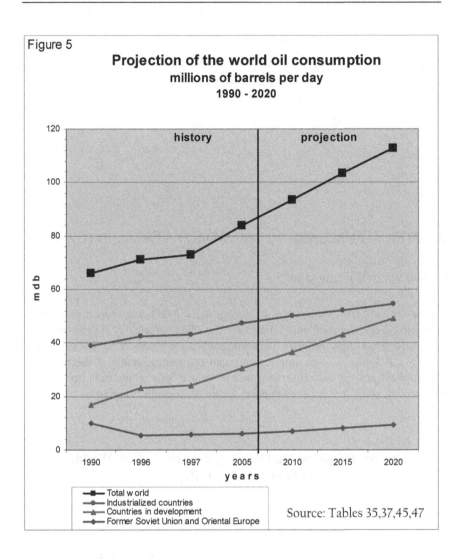

Figure 5

Projection of the world oil consumption
millions of barrels per day
1990 - 2020

Source: Tables 35,37,45,47

FUTURE CONSUMPTION: THE UNITED STATES

The United States consumption is projected to rise by 38%, from 18 million barrels/day in 1997 to 25 million barrels in 2020.

Table 36. Projected Oil Consumption, 1990-2020. United States. Millions of barrels/day.

History			Projections				Average
1990	1996	1997	2005	2010	2015	2020	
17.0	18.3	18.6	21.1	22.5	23.9	25.1	1.3

Source: Energy Information Administration. International Energy Outlook 2000.

FUTURE CONSUMPTION: RUSSIA AND THE FORMER SOVIET UNION

In these countries the consumption of petroleum will almost double, from 4.3 million barrels/day in 1997 to 7.6 million barrels/day in 2020. Starting with the breakup of the Soviet Union in 1989, the countries in the region began to consume far less, from 8.6 million per day in that year to 3.9 million barrels/day for 1999. This means that in ten years from the breakup of the Soviet Union, they reduced their consumption to less than half, which reflects the dire economic and social situation in those years. By 2020, the countries of the former Soviet Union are projected to be consuming petroleum at about the same rate as in 1989, thirty years before.

Table 37. Projected Oil Consumption, 1990-2020. Former Soviet Union. Millions of barrels/day.

History			Projections				Average
1990	1996	1997	2005	2010	2015	2020	
8.4	4.0	4.3	4.4	5.3	6.3	7.6	2.5

Source: Energy Information Administration. International Energy Outlook 2000.

FUTURE CONSUMPTION: MEXICO

Mexico is expected to increase its demand for oil more than 110%: from 1.9 millions barrels/day in 1997 to 4 million barrels in 2020.

Table 38. Projected Oil Consumption, 1990-2020. Mexico. Millions of barrels/day.

History			Projections				Average
1990	1996	1997	2005	2010	2015	2020	
1.7	1.8	1.9	2.3	2.8	3.3	4.0	3.3

Source: Energy Information Administration. International Energy Outlook 2000.

FUTURE CONSUMPTION: ASIA

The developing countries of Asia — China, India, South Korea and others — are experiencing the largest rates of growth in terms of oil consumption and may just about double their demand by 2020, to some 24.7 million barrels/day.

Table 39. Projected Oil Consumption, 1990-2020. Undeveloped Countries of Asia. Millions of barrels/day.

	History			Projections				Average
Countries	1990	1996	1997	2005	2010	2015	2020	
China	2.3	3.5	3.8	5.4	7.1	8.8	9.5	4.1
India	1.2	1.7	1.8	2.7	3.2	3.7	4.1	3.6
South Korea	1.0	2.2	2.3	2.7	3.1	3.4	3.6	2.0
Other	3.1	4.6	4.8	5.6	6.4	7.0	7.6	2.0

Source: Energy Information Administration. International Energy Outlook 2000.

FUTURE CONSUMPTION: LATIN AMERICA

It is anticipated that Latin America will double its demand from 4.4 million barrels/day in 1997 to 9.3 million barrels/day for 2020.

Table 40. Projected Oil Consumption, 1990-2020. Central and South America. Millions of barrels/day.

History			Projections				Average
1990	1996	1997	2005	2010	2015	2020	
3.4	4.2	4.4	5.4	6.5	7.8	9.3	3.4

Source: Energy Information Administration. International Energy Outlook 2000.

FUTURE CONSUMPTION: WESTERN EUROPE

Western Europe is projected to grow more slowly, from 13.8 million barrels/day to 15.3 million barrels/day.

Table 41. Projected Oil Consumption, 1990-2020. Western Europe. Millions of barrels/day.

History			Projections				Average
1990	1996	1997	2005	2010	2015	2020	
12.5	13.7	13.8	14.6	14.9	15.1	15.3	0.4

Source: Energy Information Administration. International Energy Outlook 2000.

FUTURE CONSUMPTION: INDUSTRIALIZED ASIA

The Energy Information Administration of the United States Department of Energy estimates that the industrialized countries of Asia will increase consumption from 6.9 million barrels/day in 1997 to 8.0 million barrels/day in 2020.

Table 42. Projected Oil Consumption, 1990-2020. Asia's Industrialized countries. Millions of barrels/day.

History			Projections				Average
1990	1996	1997	2005	2010	2015	2020	
6.2	7.1	6.9	7.2	7.5	7.8	8.0	0.6

Source: Energy Information Administration. International Energy Outlook 2000.

FUTURE CONSUMPTION: MIDDLE EAST

This region should double its consumption in the period studied.

Table 43. Projected oil consumption 1990-2020. Middle East. Millions of barrels/day.

History			Projections				Average
1990	1996	1997	2005	2010	2015	2020	
3.9	4.7	4.8	5.4	6.5	7.6	9	2.8

Source: Energy Information Administration. International Energy Outlook 2000.

FUTURE CONSUMPTION: AFRICA

The African continent should see one of the highest growth rates in the projected period.

Table 44. Projected Oil Consumption. 1990-2020. Africa. Millions of barrels/day.

History			Projections				Average
1990	1996	1997	2005	2010	2015	2020	
2.1	2.4	2.5	3.2	4	4.8	5.9	3.9

Source: Energy Information Administration. International Energy Outlook 2000.

CONCLUSION

The projections of the Energy Information Administration of the United States Department of Energy indicate that the rate of increase in consumption on the part of the developing countries will be triple that of the industrialized countries between 1990 and 2020, bringing them up to 49 million barrels/day. In spite of this, they won't be using as much as the industrialized countries, whose consumption is expected to be about 54.5 million barrels/day for 2020. But all the projections suggest a tremendous increase in consumption of oil worldwide between now and 2020.

Table 45. Total Projected Oil Consumption: Industrial Countries. 1990-2020. Millions of barrels/day.

History			Projections				Average
1990	1996	1997	2005	2010	2015	2020	
39	42,6	43,1	47,3	49,9	52,3	54,5	1,0

Source: Energy Information Administration. International Energy Outlook 2000.

Table 46. Total Projected Oil Consumption: Undeveloped Countries. 1990-2020. Millions of barrels/day.

History			Projections				Average
1990	1996	1997	2005	2010	2015	2020	
17.0	23.3	24.2	30.6	36.6	43.0	49.0	3.1

Source: Energy Information Administration International Energy. Outlook 2000.

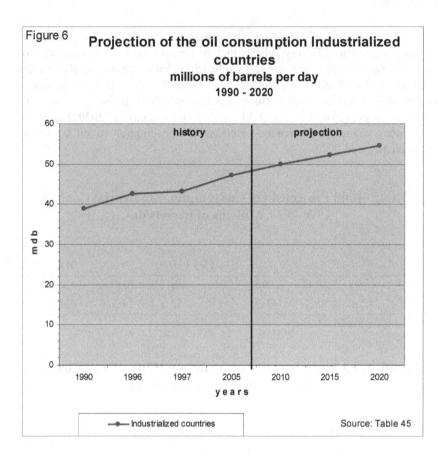

Figure 6

Projection of the oil consumption Industrialized countries
millions of barrels per day
1990 - 2020

Source: Table 45

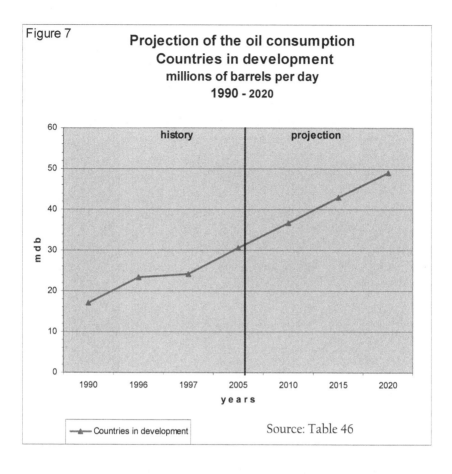

Figure 7

**Projection of the oil consumption
Countries in development**
millions of barrels per day
1990 - 2020

Source: Table 46

CHAPTER 8. MORE PRODUCTION, LESS RESERVES

Until the start of the second Arab oil embargo, oil production grew steadily. Starting in 1974, production began to fluctuate, although there were no significant dips.

In the 1940s, production grew at an average rate of 6.1%.

Table 47. Crude Oil Production. Total World. 1940s.
Thousands of barrels/day.

Year	Production	% Change
1940	5,890	
1941	6,084	3.3
1942	5,735	-5.7
1943	6,183	7.8
1944	7,102	14.9
1945	7,109	0.1
1946	7,522	5.8
1947	8,280	10.1
1948	9,406	13.6
1949	9,326	-0.9
1950	10,419	11.7
	Average Growth of Production	
	6.1	

Source: Oil Facts and Figures. 1971 Edition. American Oil Institute. P. 548

In 1940, for example, worldwide production reached 5.8 million barrels a day. Ten years later, it was almost double. In another five years, it reached 15.4

million barrels a day, an increase of 48%. By 1960, production had been doubled again to 21 million barrels/day.

Table 48. Crude Oil Production. World. 1950s.
Thousands of barrels/day.

Years	Production	% Change
1950	10,419	
1951	11,734	12.6
1952	12,414	5.8
1953	13,145	5.9
1954	13,745	4.6
1955	15,413	12.1
1956	16,779	8.9
1957	17,645	5.2
1958	18,129	2.7
1959	19,543	7.8
1960	21,026	7.6
	Average Growth of Production	
	7.3	

Source: Oil Facts and Figures. 1971 Edition. American Oil Institute. P. 548

In the 1960s, the known reserves grew on average 6.6% per year, less than the average growth in production (8%). We were already spending more than we were taking in.

Table 49. Crude Oil Production, Reserves and Consumption of Refined Products. World. 1960s.

Years	Production	% Change	Reserves	% Change	Consump- tion	% Change
	thousands of barrels/day		*millions of barrels*		*thousands of barrels/day*	
1960	20,934		291,167		19,829	
1961	22,343	6.7	297,481	2.2	21,106	6.4
1962	24,263	8.6	310,673	4.4	22,845	8.2
1963	25,960	7.0	332,396	7.0	24,650	7.9
1964	28,071	8.1	342,516	3.0	26,651	8.1
1965	30,201	7.6	353,218	3.1	28,741	7.8
1966	32,812	8.6	388,616	10.0	31,005	7.9
1967	35,291	7.6	410,896	5.7	33,323	7.5
1968	38,054	7.8	463,736	12.9	36,417	9.3
1969	41,246	8.4	534,219	15.2	39,640	8.9
1970	45,272	9.8	549,735	2.9	43,451	9.6
	Average Growth of Production		Average Growth of Reserves		Average Growth of Consumption	
	8.00		6.6		8.2	

Source: OPEC Annual Statistical Bulletin 1989.

In 1970, world oil production was in 45.2 million barrels/day. The reserves grew an average of 2% while production was boosted by 2.9%. Some countries nationalized the international oil companies in the 1970s. Up to then, to avoid paying taxes, some oil companies had been underestimating the oil reserves in the areas where they operated. This situation is reflected in the increase in reported reserves that is observed in the following decade.

Table 50. Crude Oil Production, Reserves and Consumption of Refined Products. World. 1970s.

Years	Production	% Change	Reserves	% Change	Consumption	% Change
	thousands of barrels/day		*million barrels*		*thousands of barrels/day*	
1970	45,272		549,735		43,451	
1971	47,854	5.7	569,826	3.7	46,040	6.0
1972	50,708	6.0	579,867	1.8	49,691	7.9
1973	55,478	9.4	580,495	0.1	53,638	7.9
1974	55,813	0.6	654,102	12.7	52,799	-1.6
1975	52,746	-5.5	624,577	-4.5	52,170	-1.2
1976	57,566	9.1	612,350	-2.0	55,849	7.1
1977	59,806	3.9	617,508	0.8	58,211	4.2
1978	60,265	0.8	621,895	0.7	60,662	4.2
1979	62,800	4.2	631,595	1.6	61,725	1.8
1980	59,767	-4.8	664,709	5.2	59,277	-4.0
	Average Growth of Production		Average Growth of Reserves		Average Growth of Consumption	
	2.9		2.0		3.2	

Sources: OPEC Annual Statistical Bulletin 1981; 1982; 1989; 1990.
Oil and Gas Journal 1999. Energy Statistics Sourcebook.

In the 1980s, the reserves/production ration was briefly turned around and the reported reserves grew by an average of 4.4% while production growth hovered at the very modest figure of 0.2%. This phenomenon, as noted, is explained in part by the nationalization of some oil facilities, with the new owners, the governments, more accurately reporting the state of their reserves. At the same time, countries with the greatest need for oil redoubled their efforts to find new sources, to accumulate strategic reserves, and to reduce consumption, objectives which they partially achieved.

Table 51. Crude Oil Production, Reserves and Consumption of Refined Products. World. 1980s.

Years	Production	% Change	Reserves	% Change	Consump-tion	% Change
	thousands of barrels/day		*millions barrels*		*thousands of barrels/day*	
1980	59,767		664,709		59,277	
1981	56,027	-6.3	676,747	1.8	57,200	-3.5
1982	53,739	-4.1	703,483	4.0	55,926	-2.2
1983	52,803	-1.7	708,512	0.7	57,780	3.3
1984	53,118	0.6	742,405	4.8	56,304	-2.6
1985	53,291	0.3	741,237	-0.2	56,025	-0.5
1986	56,289	5.6	858,921	15.9	56,796	1.4
1987	55,377	-1.6	890,761	3.7	58,008	2.1
1988	57,863	4.5	994,391	11.6	59,650	2.8
1989	58,637	1.3	1,009,040	1.5	60,575	1.6
1990	60,384	3.0	1,012,046	0.3	60,005	-0.9
	Average Growth of Production		Average Growth of Reserves		Average Growth of Consumption	
	0.2		4.4		0.1	

Source: *OPEC Annual Statistical Bulletin 1982; 1984; 1985; 1989; 1999; 2000.*

But in the last ten years of the 20th century, the reserves showed signs of deterioration again, this time a sharp deterioration. Great faith had been placed in future discoveries, when as-yet-uninvented technologies would enable us to keep on finding and accessing presumed reserves in more remote places, such as under the deep layer of salt in the Gulf of Mexico. Some such innovations have indeed been put in place, but production and consumption continue to be increased faster than new discoveries are made; we are simply reducing the total resources.

The figures show that the rate at which production was growing exceeded the rate at which the reserves grew during the 1990s, which tends to confirm that the supply is getting tighter. While production worldwide was stepped up by an average of 0.9%, the reserves grew at only 0.6%. This is stagnation, at best.

Table 52. Crude Oil Production, Reserves and Consumption of Refined Products. World. 1990s.

Years	Production	% Change	Reserves	% Change	Consump- tion	% Change
	thousands of barrels/day		*million barrels*		*thousands of barrels/day*	
1990	60,384		1,012,046		60,005	
1991	59,069	-2.2	1,005,505	-0.6	60,868	1.4
1992	59,752	1.2	1,007,382	0.2	60,963	0.2
1993	59,312	-0.7	1,009,819	0.2	61,098	0.2
1994	60,007	1.2	1,019,535	1.0	61,860	1.2
1995	60,520	0.9	1,025,549	0.6	62,829	1.6
1996	61,433	1.5	1,049,590	2.3	66,355	5.6
1997	62,853	2.3	1,052,508	0.3	68,081	2.6
1998	65,012	3.4	1,057,853	0.5	68,539	0.7
1999	63,368	-2.5	1,048,229	-0.9	69,926	2.0
2000	65,824	3.9	1,077,499	2.8	70,595	1.0
	Average Growth of Production		Average Growth of Reserves		Average Growth of Consumption	
	0.9		0.6		1.6	

Source: OPEC Annual Statistical Bulletin 1990; 1995; 1999; 2000

How long will the proven oil reserves last? Table 53 looks at reserves versus production.

Table 53. Projected Lifetime of Proven Reserves of Crude Oil. World. 1960-2000.

Years	Production	Reserves	
	thousands of barrels/day	*millions barrels*	*duration in years*
1960	20,934	291,167	38.1
1961	22,343	297,481	36.5
1962	24,263	310,673	35.1
1963	25,960	332,396	35.1
1964	28,071	342,516	33.4
1965	30,201	353,218	32.0
1966	32,812	388,616	32.4
1967	35,291	410,896	31.9
1968	38,054	463,736	33.4
1969	41,246	534,219	35.5
1970	45,272	549,735	33.3
1971	47,854	569,826	32.6
1972	50,708	579,867	31.3
1973	55,478	580,495	28.7
1974	55,813	654,102	32.1
1975	52,746	624,577	32.4
1976	57,566	612,350	29.1
1977	59,806	617,508	28.3
1978	60,265	621,895	28.3
1979	62,800	631,595	27.6
1980	59,767	664,709	30.5
1980	59,767	664,709	30.5
1981	56,027	676,747	33.1
1982	53,739	703,483	35.9
1983	52,803	708,512	36.8
1984	53,118	742,405	38.3
1985	53,291	741,237	38.1
1986	56,289	858,921	41.8
1987	55,377	890,761	44.1
1988	57,863	994,391	47.1
1989	58,637	1,009,040	47.1
1990	60,384	1,012,046	45.9
1991	59,069	1,005,505	46.6
1992	59,752	1,007,382	46.2
1993	59,312	1,009,819	46.6
1994	60,007	1,019,535	46.5

1995	60,520	1,025,549	46.4
1996	61,433	1,049,590	46.8
1997	62,853	1,052,508	45.9
1998	65,012	1,057,853	44.6
1999	63,368	1,048,229	45.3
2000	65,824	1,077,499	44.8

Source: OPEC Annual Statistical Bulletin 1990; 1995; 1999; 2000

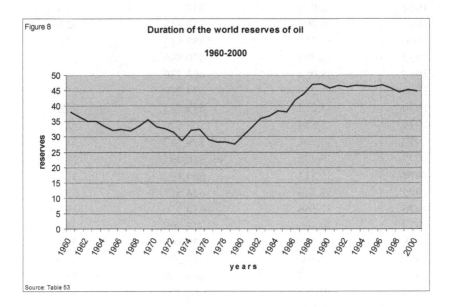

Figure 8 — **Duration of the world reserves of oil 1960-2000**

Source: Table 53

It could also be argued that the growth of the reserves in the 1980s was linked to the high price of oil in those years. That seems logical, in that higher prices discourage consumption and encourage exploration and drilling by increasing oil company profits, but it does not explain why reserves grew from the beginning of oil exploitation in 1860 until the 1970s, when the whole period was characterized by low and stable oil prices. The year 1973 was the first time that the trend of low and stable prices was broken.

Rather, the high prices of the 1980s in conjunction with both the advent of new technologies and the political decision of the oil countries to report their reserves more accurately — creating a more or less artificial boost compared to the picture that had been presented previously by the international oil companies — could explain why the reserves "grew" in this decade.

In the 1990s, the trend toward stagnation in the world's oil reserves was more clear. In recent years, there has been very little progress in discovering "new" oil layers. It begins to seem that there is not a lot of oil left to be found.

Some people have a tendency to spend more than they earn. However, when it comes to petroleum, there is no gift or inheritance to wait for and we are, in essence, mortgaging our future. Simple arithmetic shows that we cannot go on forever taking out more than we out into the system. If you take out more money than you deposit in your account, you are driving yourself into poverty. The difference between what you take out and what you deposit has to come from somewhere, either from the reserves you had in another account or from some other valuables that you can sell. If you continue to maintain a high expense level, the time will come when you have used up all your resources. Yet, that is just what is going on with oil. Every day, the world burns as much as it has discovered. The only exception was in the 1980s; and in the following decade, the situation was completely the contrary.

At this rate, the next oil shock will be more shocking than anything we've seen — and brought on largely by man's heedlessness.

THE SAME HOLDS TRUE FOR COAL

But it's not only oil reserves that are failing to increase in pace with demand. Coal reserves have diminished too, as shown in Table 54.

Table 54. Proven Reserves of Mineral Coal. World. 1990s.

Years	Reserves	% Change
	billions of tons	
1990	1,075.1	—
1991	—	—
1992	1,042.9	—
1993	1,044.4	0.1
1994	1,049.2	0.5
1995	1,038.9	-1.0
1996	1,041.6	0.3
1997	1,040.6	-0.1
1999	977.6	0.0
2000	984.2	0.7
	Average Growth of production	
	-0.7	

Sources: *Statistical and Energy Economic Indicators of Latin America and the Caribbean, November 2000. Latin American Organization of Energy. OLADE. P. 3. B.P. Statistical Review of World Energy 2001.*

CONSUMPTION OF PRIMARY ENERGY

In 1999, oil was the principal energy source on a global scale, accounting from some 36.8% of consumption; coal accounted for 32.3%, natural gas 20.5%, biomass 6.3 and other forms of electricity generation 4.1% of the total consumption of primary energy.

Table 55. Consumption of Primary Energy. World. 1999.

Sources of Energy	Millions of BEP *	% of the Total
Oil	24,921	36.8
Natural gas	13,918	20.5
Electricity (**)	2,775	4.1
Coal	21,889	32.3
Biomass	4,264	6.3
Total	67,767	100.0

*BEP: equivalent barrels of oil.
**Electricity = Hydroelectricity+geoelectricity+ nuclear energy.
Source: Statistical and Energy Economic Indicators of Latin America and the Caribbean, November 2000. Latin American Energy Organization (OLADE), p. 7.

ENERGY CONSUMPTION IN LATIN AMERICA

The transportation sector uses the largest percentage of petroleum as an energy source, followed by industry. These two sectors represent around 70% of the oil consumption in Latin America.

Table 56. Energy Consumption by Sector. Latin America and the Caribbean. 1999.

Sectors	Thousands of equivalent barrels of oil	% of Total
Transport	1,028,945	35.4
Industry	1,006,604	34.6
Residential, Commercial, Public Services	588,624	20.2
Agriculture, Fisheries, Mining, Construction, Other	145,136	5.0
Not energy	141,112	4.8
Total	2,910,421	100.0

Sources: Statistical and Energy Economic Indicators of Latin America and the Caribbean, November 2000. Latin American Energy Organization (OLADE), p. 33.

CHAPTER 9. CRUDE OIL IN THE NON-OPEC COUNTRIES

THE UNITED STATES AND HUBBERT'S CURVE

Assuming the past can help predict the future, the geologist M. King Hubbert made some calculations as to the future of oil in the United States — in 1956, when oil production in the United States was booming. Hubbert predicted that this country would reach its maximum production in 1969 and then begin to decline. Hubbert observed at the time that the amount of new reserves discovered in the United States was not keeping pace with the production figures and that difference is the basis of his theory.

Of course, his predictions were not taken seriously at the time, but later, in 1970, almost on schedule, his forecast was proven right.

The United States: Oil Production, Reserves and Consumption 1940-2000

In the 1940s the United States saw a 4% growth in oil production, on average, which is a pretty good figure. The world was undergoing big changes at the time. The most remarkable was World War II, which lasted from the beginning of the decade to 1945. In those years, the energy needs of the world multiplied and were met, largely, with oil. The reserves grew at just 2.9% per annum.

Table 57. The United States. Crude Oil Production and Reserves. 1940s.

Years	Production	% Change	Reserves	% Change
	thousands of barrels/day		*millions of barrels*	
1940	3,707		19,024	
1941	3,841	3.6	19,589	3.0
1942	3,799	-1.1	20,082	2.5
1943	4,124	8.6	20,064	-0.1
1944	4,596	11.5	20,453	1.9
1945	4,694	2.1	20,826	1.8
1946	4,750	1.2	20,873	0.2
1947	5,087	7.1	21,487	2.9
1948	5,534	8.8	23,280	8.3
1949	5,046	-8.8	24,649	5.9
1950	5,407	7.2	25,268	2.5
	Average Growth of production		Average Growth of reserves	
	4.0		2.9	

Source: Oil Facts and Figures. 1959 and 1971 Editions. American Oil Institute. Pages 110, 548.

In the 1950s, oil production in the United States grew at a more measured pace, 2.8%. In this decade the reconstruction efforts in Europe and the rest of the world drove a construction boom, and reserves grew at a slightly slower rate than production.

Table 58. The United States. Crude Oil Production and Reserves. 1950s.

Years	Production	% Change	Reserves	% Change
	thousands of barrels/ day		millions of barrels	
1950	5,407		25,268	
1951	6,158	13.9	27,468	8.7
1952	6,273	1.9	27,960	1.8
1953	6,457	2.9	28,944	3.5
1954	6,342	-1.8	29,560	2.1
1955	6,806	7.3	30,012	1.5
1956	7,170	5.4	30,434	1.4
1957	7,169	0.0	30,300	-0.4
1958	6,709	-6.4	30,535	0.8
1959	7,053	5.1	31,719	3.9
1960	7,054	0.0	31,613	-0.3
	Average Growth of Production		Average Growth of Reserves	
	2.8		2.3	

Source: *Oil Facts and Figures. 1959 and 1971 Editions. American Oil Institute. Page 110; 548.*

In the 1960s, North American oil production picked up speed and it grew on average at 3.2%. The 1960s were also characterized by the beginning of a new war for the United States. The war in Vietnam meant big sacrifices in lives and in material terms. North American oil production grew sharply from 7 million barrels/day in 1960 to 9.6 million barrels/day in 1970; reserves grew far more slowly.

Table 59. The United States. Crude Oil Production and Reserves. 1960s.

Years	Production	% Change	Reserves	% Change
	thousands of barrels/day		*millions of barrels*	
1960	7,054		31,613	
1961	7,182	1.8	31,758	0.5
1962	7,332	2.1	31,389	-1.2
1963	7,541	2.9	30,969	-1.3
1964	7,635	1.2	30,990	0.1
1965	7,804	2.2	31,352	1.2
1966	8,295	6.3	31,452	0.3
1967	8,810	6.2	31,376	-0.2
1968	9,120	3.5	30,707	-2.1
1969	9,210	1.0	29,631	-3.5
1970	9,630	4.6	29,631	0.0
	Average Growth of Production		Average Growth of Reserves	
	3.2		-0.6	

Source: Oil Facts and Figures. 1959 and 1971 Editions. American Oil Institute. Page 110; 548.

As noted, the US reached its highest level of oil production, 9.6 million barrels/day, in 1970 and in 1971 it achieved the maximum level of reserves in the second half of the 20th century: 39,001 million barrels. Since then, both sides of the equation have been going down.

Table 60. The United States. Crude Oil Production, Reserves and Consumption of Refined Products. 1970s.

	Production	% Change	Reserves	% Change	Consumption	% Change
	thousands of barrels/ day		*millions of barrels*		*thousands of barrels/day*	
1970	9,630		29,631		14,350	
1971	9,529	-1.0	39,001	31.6	14,830	3.3
1972	9,451	-0.8	38,062	-2.4	15,980	7.8
1973	9,189	-2.8	36,339	-4.5	17,305	8.3
1974	8,812	-4.1	35,299	-2.9	16,745	-3.2
1975	8,351	-5.2	34,249	-3.0	16,243	-3.0
1976	8,114	-2.8	32,682	-4.6	16,980	4.5
1977	8,240	1.6	30,942	-5.3	18,431	8.5
1978	8,670	5.2	29,486	-4.7	18,846	2.3
1979	8,678	0.1	27,803	-5.7	18,513	-1.8
1980	8,569	-1.3	27,051	-2.7	17,056	-7.9
	Average Growth of Production		Average Growth of Reserves		Average Growth of Consumption	
	-1.1		-0.4		1.9	

Sources: *International Encyclopedia 1978. Oil and Gas Journal 1999. Energy Statistics Sourcebook. P. 156. OPEC Annual Statistical Bulletin 1982.*

In the 1980s, oil production in the United States continued its descent, falling from 8.5 million barrels/day in 1980 to 7.2 million barrels/day in 1990. The reserves presented an average decrease of 0.3% and consumption fell by 0.9%.

Table 61. The United States. Crude Oil Production, Reserves and Consumption of Refined Products. 1980s.

Years	Production	% Change	Reserves	% Change	Consumption	% Change
	thousands of barrels/day		*millions of barrels*		*thousands of barrels/day*	
1980	8,569		27,051		17,056	
1981	8,554	-0.2	29,426	8.8	14,997	-12.1
1982	8,660	1.2	27,858	-5.3	14,155	-5.6
1983	8,687	0.3	27,735	-0.4	14,095	-0.4
1984	8,735	0.6	28,446	2.6	14,360	1.9
1985	8,971	2.7	28,000	-1.6	14,273	-0.6
1986	8,680	-3.2	26,889	-4.0	14,841	4.0
1987	8,349	-3.8	27,256	1.4	15,305	3.1
1988	8,096	-3.0	26,825	-1.6	15,791	3.2
1989	7,565	-6.6	26,501	-1.2	15,744	-0.3
1990	7,226	-4.5	26,145	-1.3	15,366	-2.4
	Average Growth of Production		Average Growth of Reserves		Average Growth of Consumption	
	-1.6		-0.3		-0.9	

Source: OPEC Annual Statistical Bulletin 1982; 1984; 1985; 1989; 1990; 1995.

In the 1990s American reserves shrank by an average of -1.8%, from 26.1 million barrels in 1990 to 21.7 million barrels in 2000 (bringing US reserves down to a level similar to what it had in 1947). Thus, the amount of oil in all the new reserves that had been found since 1947 had already been consumed in that period. No net gain.

Table 62. The United States. Crude Oil Reserves, Production and Consumption of Refined Products. 1990s.

Years	Production	% Change	Reserves	% Change	Consump- tion	% Change
	thousands of barrels/ day		*millions of barrels*		*thousands of barrels/day*	
1990	7,226		26,145		15,366	
1991	7,416	2.6	24,682	-5.6	15,434	0.4
1992	7,171	-3.3	23,745	-3.8	15,642	1.3
1993	6,846	-4.5	22,957	-3.3	15,865	1.4
1994	6,661	-2.7	22,457	-2.2	16,340	3.0
1995	6,558	-1.5	22,351	-0.5	16,730	2.4
1996	6,465	-1.4	22,017	-1.5	17,221	2.9
1997	6,451	-0.2	22,017	0.0	17,529	1.8
1998	6,252	-3.1	22,546	2.4	17,861	1.9
1999	5,881	-5.9	21,034	-6.7	18,489	3.5
2000	5,821	-1.0	21,765	3.5	18,656	0.9
	Average Growth of Production		Average Growth of Reserves		Average Growth of Consumption	
	-2.1		-1.8		2.0	

Source: OPEC Annual Statistical Bulletin 1990; 1995; 1999, 2000.

CONCLUSION ON THE UNITED STATES

American oil production always moved upward until 1970, when production reached a peak at 9.6 million barrels/day. Starting then, a sustained downward trend began; it continued in the 1990s until it reached 5.8 million barrels/day for the year 2000. That is similar to the US level of production in 1950.

There's No Guarantee of New Reserves

The fact that we keep coming up with new technologies does not guarantee the discovery of new oil reserves. Sooner or later, there will be no more reserves to discover, whatever the technology. Already in the 1990s, when oil companies had the best technology in history, reserves did not increase as much as expected. Based on Hubbert's Curve, some experts have estimated that demand for oil will outstrip supply in the next few years, and therefore the reserves will not recover.

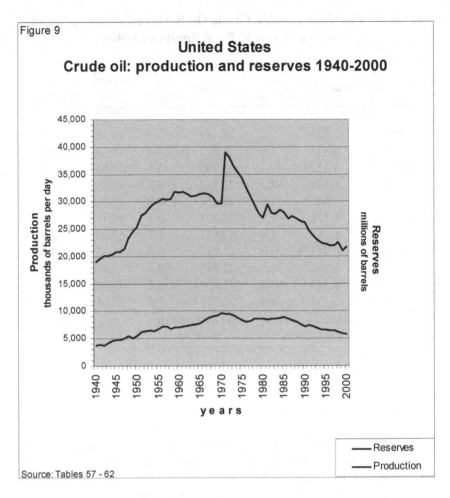

Figure 9

**United States
Crude oil: production and reserves 1940-2000**

Source: Tables 57 - 62

The Beginning of the End

Hubbert maintained that the production curve of non-renewable natural resources begins at zero and extends to a maximum point at which it inevitably begins to fall. Hubbert made his projection in relation to the United States and it was fulfilled. He asserted that when 50% of the reserves of one oil field have been depleted, inevitably the process of its decline begins; therefore, one can predict how much longer the production of that field will last. Today there are methods — like the seismic method of production — to test whether the halfway point has been reached in a given field. Now geologists, applying the Hubbert thesis, have verified that this is happening right now in Russia and the same thing will happen very soon in other regions of the world.

Experts predicted that some countries would reach their maximum point of oil production between 2000 and 2001 but the truth is that this process began in the 1970s. The North Sea, for example, reached it between 1996 and 1997, when it produced more than 5 million barrels/day. Saudi Arabia reached its production peak of 9.9 millions barrels/day in 1980 and has never yet repeated that performance. Venezuela reached its peak of 3.7 million barrels/day in 1970 and Mexico hit 3 million barrels/day in 2000, as shown in Chapters 9 and 10. Mexico, United Kingdom and Norway are also confronting problems because of the decline of its fields and the same thing will happen very soon with conventional oil in Venezuela.

The proven reserves in Venezuela reached 27,200 million barrels in 1985. The following year this country doubled its reserves to 55,500 million barrels (see Table 125). But this was accomplished by including part of the nonconventional oil in the Orinoco Belt reserves, which shows that in reality Venezuelan reserves of conventional oil were and are very low. According to the official figures of the Venezuelan Energy and Mines Ministry[26] the proven reserves reached 73,685 million barrels for 2000. Of this quantity, 32,918 million barrels are extra heavy crude and 2,769 million barrels are bitumen; this means that almost half of the Venezuela proven reserves for the year 2000 corresponded to nonconventional crude, the processing of which requires a greater financial and technical effort.

Venezuela has the greatest world reserves of nonconventional oil, in the Orinoco Belt, an area where they are having some success in transforming the nonconventional oil into light oil. The great question is when Venezuela will be able to use all of those reserves. The answer to that question is important because it would mean an important contribution to the world's reserves.

Calculating the Productive Life of an Oilfield

Starting from the principle that all non-renewable resources have a certain level of reserves that can be exploited over time, the world's oil companies have always made their calculations of the useful lifetime of their fields using an equation reflecting time and production rates. The equation is very simple: the horizontal line represents time and the vertical line, production. Production is represented by a group of points that start at coordinate zero and go up until arriving at a high point level from which it inevitably begins to decline. The curve can be prolonged over a longer time period, but it has to come down sooner or later. The downward curve in oil production can be attenuated with secondary and tertiary recovery projects. The production of a field can be prolonged by up

---

26. Venezuela Energy and Mines Ministry, Oil and Natural Gas Reserves at December 31 2000, tables 4 and 12, Hydrocarbons General Direction.

to 25% of the original production or more. But the end eventually comes. This is inevitable.

THE HUBBERT METHOD

It is the same Hubbert equation that international oil companies use to calculate the useful lifetime of their fields. One may infer that if the method is good enough for calculating the useful life of each field, it is equally useful in making broader projections. If it is good enough to determine the lifetime of one field, it is good enough to determine the lifetime of many fields, to calculate the situation in a region and also in the whole world. Observing the behavior of worldwide production and reserves in time, you can find the moment at which the various countries have reached their peak production and their peak of reserves, and then you can infer when they might enter the following decline phase: as has happened in the United States and in Russia.

The Decline of the Fields

The oilfields are not eternal. They have a time of birth, splendor and death. The decline of the oilfields in the major oil producer countries is a reality. Not only is very little "new" oil being discovered, but the fields currently in production are also reaching their peaks, which necessarily leads to the beginning of the period of their exhaustion.

This is what is happening in the North Sea, where production reached its maximum point and the experts estimated that it would begin to decline in 2005. Official reports on the topic confirm that estimate. Indeed, the *Financial Times* of June 27, 2001, highlighted an official report according to which the United Kingdom will become in an importer of oil by 2006–2007, after being self-sufficient since the 1970s. Norway also taps the North Sea resources. Both are important non-OPEC countries that have contributed significantly to the supply of oil in recent decades, but they are beginning to face serious production problems.

The North Sea made a significant contribution to oil production since it came online in the 1970s. In 2000, Norway contributed 3.1 million barrels/day and the United Kingdom 2.3 million barrels/day. That total of 5.4 million barrels/day represented 8.2% of the daily world production.[27] The retirement from the market of the North Sea as a producer would leave an important gap that will have to be filled by other regions. It is obvious that this will affect world prices and will have political and economic effects not only for the United Kingdom

---

27. OPEC Annual Statistical Bulletin 2000.

and Norway, but for the other producers — and consumers as well. In the medium term, in this first decade of the 21st century, the deterioration of North Sea production can only intensify the smoldering oil-supply crisis.

THE UNITED KINGDOM

The Arab oil embargo in 1973 drove prices through the roof. With the new prices, production that had been uneconomical until then, in certain countries and regions like the North Sea, became profitable. The higher revenues and the need to reduce dependence on OPEC favored the development of the North Sea oil fields. Between 1970 and 1974, production in the United Kingdom was minimal: only 2,000 barrels/day. But starting in 1975, the oilfields of the North Sea came into production and Great Britain's oil production shot upward: 241,000 barrels in 1976; 767,000 barrels/day in 1977; a million barrels/day in 1978; a million and half in 1979 until reaching a million 600,000 barrels in 1980. The United Kingdom reached its highest level of reserves, 19 billion barrels, in 1978. The advent of the United Kingdom as an oil producer represented an important change in global oil politics, because the volume of its production provided the West with some energy security by reducing consumer nations' OPEC dependence.

Table 63. The United Kingdom. Crude Oil Production and Reserves. 1970s.

Years	Production	% Change	Reserves	% Change
	thousands of barrels/day		*millions of barrels*	
1970	1.9		7	
1971	1.6	-15.8	1,000	14,185.7
1972	1.6	0.0	5,000	400.0
1973	2.0	25.0	5,000	0.0
1974	2.0	0.0	10,000	100.0
1975	19.0	850.0	15,700	57.0
1976	241	1,168.4	16,000	1.9
1977	767	218.3	16,800	5.0
1978	1,081	40.9	19,000	13.1
1979	1,567	45.0	16,000	-15.8
1980	1,619	3.3	15,400	-3.8
	Average Growth of Production		Average Growth of Reserves	
	233.5		147.4	

Sources: *OPEC Annual Statistical Bulletin 1982; 1984; 1985; 1989; 1990; 1999. Oil and Gas Journal 1999. Energy Statistics Sourcebook. P. 153, 156.*

In the 1980s, production maintained its growth rate, reaching 2.5 million barrels/day in 1985. But the reserves were already falling. Indeed, in only ten years the reserves decreased by 74%.

Table 64. The United Kingdom. Crude Oil Production, Reserves and Consumption of Refined Products. 1980s.

Years	Production	% Change	Reserves	% Change	Consumption	% Change
	thousands of barrels/day		*Millions of barrels*		*thousands of barrels/day*	
1980	1,619		15,400			
1981	1,800	11.2	7,825	-49.2	1,383	
1982	2,100	16.7	7,448	-4.8	1,425	3.0
1983	2,300	9.5	6,960	-6.6	1,368	-4.0
1984	2,476	7.7	6,015	-13.6	1,657	21.1
1985	2,514	1.5	5,663	-5.9	1,426	-13.9
1986	2,493	-0.8	5,310	-6.2	1,488	4.3
1987	2,062	-17.3	5,137	-3.3	1,441	-3.2
1988	2,142	3.9	4,275	-16.8	1,517	5.3
1989	1,791	-16.4	4,255	-0.5	1,543	1.7
1990	1,799	0.4	3,825	-10.1	1,549	0.4
	Average Growth of Production		Average Growth of Reserves		Average Growth of Consumption	
	1.6		-11.7		1.6	

Source: OPEC Annual Statistical Bulletin 1982; 1984; 1985; 1989; 1990; 1995; 1999.

In the 1990s, production continued to go up, reaching the figure of 2.5 million barrels/day in 1999, the highest level Great Britain reached in its history as a producer. The reserves did grow, to a maximum level of 19 billion barrels in 1978, but production grew far faster so that, if the trend holds, this country will very soon shift from being an exporter to a net importer of oil. The United Kingdom's proven reserves fell to 5 billion barrels in 2000; quite a hefty decrease.

Table 65. The United Kingdom. Crude Oil Production, Reserves and Consumption of Refined Products. 1990s.

Years	Production	% Change	Reserves	% Change	Consumption	% Change
	thousands of barrels/day		*millions of barrels*		*thousands of barrels/day*	
1990	1,799		3,825		1,549	
1991	1,793	-0.3	3,994	4.4	1,580	2.0
1992	1,883	5.0	4,141	3.7	1,562	-1.1
1993	1,987	5.5	4,554	10.0	1,545	-1.1
1994	2,396	20.6	4,516	-0.8	1,563	1.2
1995	2,420	1.0	4,293	-4.9	1,732	10.8
1996	2,418	-0.1	4,516	5.2	1,768	2.1
1997	2,422	0.2	5,002	10.8	1,710	-3.3
1998	2,506	3.5	5,190	3.8	1,701	-0.5
1999	2,569	2.5	5,153	-0.7	1,695	-0.4
2000	2,378	-7.4	5,002	-2.9	1,667	-1.7
	Average Growth of Production		Average Growth of Reserves		Average Growth of Consumption	
	3.0		2.8		0.7	

Source: OPEC Annual Statistical Bulletin 1982; 1984; 1985; 1989; 1990; 1995; 1999; 2000.

105

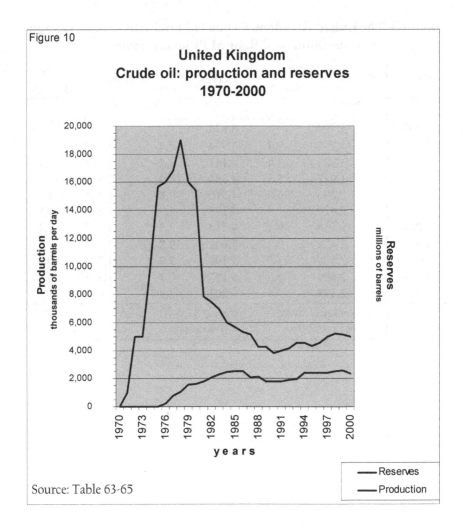

Figure 10

United Kingdom
Crude oil: production and reserves
1970-2000

Source: Table 63-65

NORWAY

Norway is in a similar bind. Norway had not produced a drop of oil before 1970. But in 1971, production began at 12,000 barrels/day; the next year it reached 33,000 barrels/day. But in 1975 the momentum grew and Norway began to produce 188,000 barrels/day, a figure that then increased until it reached 556,000 barrels/day in 1980. The reserves also grew in this decade, from 1 billion barrels in 1971 to 5.7 billion barrels in 1980, a significant growth.

Table 66. Norway. Crude Oil Production and Reserves. 1970s.

Years	Production	% Change	Reserves	% Change
	thousands of barrels/day		*millions of barrels*	
1970				
1971	12		1,000	
1972	33	175.0	7,000	600.0
1973	33	0.0	2,000	-71.4
1974	34	3.0	4,000	100.0
1975	188	452.9	7,300	82.5
1976	278	47.9	7,000	-4.1
1977	279	0.4	5,660	-19.1
1978	355	27.2	6,000	6.0
1979	403	13.5	5,900	-1.7
1980	556	38.0	5,750	-2.5
	Average Growth of Production		Average Growth of Reserves	
	84.2		76.6	

Sources: OPEC Annual Statistical Bulletin 1970, 1980. Oil and Gas Journal 1999. Energy Statistics Sourcebook. P. 162.

Production surpassed one million barrels/day in 1987. The reserves also expanded significantly, tripling from 5.7 billion barrels in 1980 to 15.6 billion barrels in 1990. This was the high point in Norway's reserves.

In the 1990s, Norway accelerated its oil production and reached the impressive figure of 3.1 million barrels/day in 2000, the greatest production in all its history. But in this decade the reserves began to decline, from 16.6 billion barrels in 1990 to 13.1 billion barrels in 2000. If this production growth rate, averaging 6.7%, is compared with the growth rate of the reserves, -0.4%, it is clear that this country's oil is being exhausted.

Table 67. Norway. Crude Oil Production and Reserves. 1980s.

Years	Production	% Change	Reserves	% Change
	thousands of barrels/day		*millions of barrels*	
1980	526		5,750	
1981	473	-1.1	7,620	32.5
1982	530	12.1	6,800	-10.8
1983	656	23.8	7,660	12.6
1984	693	5.6	8,300	8.4
1985	771	11.3	10,900	31.3
1986	888	15.2	10,500	-3.7
1987	1,029	15.9	11,076	5.5
1988	1,173	14.0	11,038	-0.3
1989	1,175	0.2	15,626	41.6
1990	1,685	43.4	15,608	-0.1
	Average Growth of Production		Average Growth of Reserves	
	13.1		11.7	

Source: OPEC Annual Statistical Bulletin 1984; 1885; 1989; 1990.

Table 68. Norway. Crude Oil Production and Reserves. 1990s.

Years	Production	% Change	Reserves	% Change
	thousands of barrels/day		*millions of barrels*	
1990	1,685		16,608	
1991	1,882	11.7	9,894	-40.4
1992	2,102	11.7	10,122	2.3
1993	2,268	7.9	10,194	0.7
1994	2,538	11.9	12,277	20.4
1995	2,697	6.3	13,612	10.9
1996	3,030	12.3	11,280	-17.1
1997	3,062	1.1	10,913	-3.3
1998	2,908	-5.0	10,366	-5.0
1999	2,921	0.4	13,485	30.1
2000	3,182	8.9	13,158	-2.4
	Average Growth of Production		Average Growth of Reserves	
	6.7		-0.4	

Source: OPEC Annual Statistical Bulletin 1990; 1995; 1999; 2000.

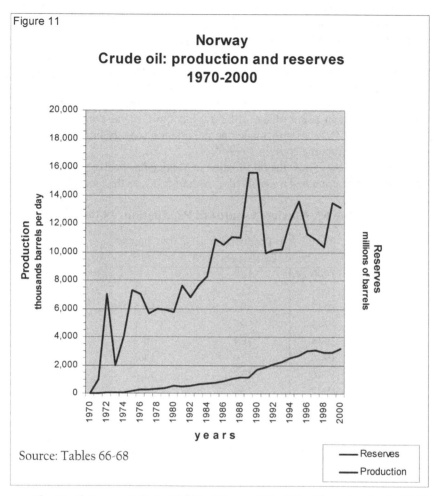

Figure 11

Norway
Crude oil: production and reserves
1970-2000

Source: Tables 66-68

The North Sea contributed 8.2% of the world's daily oil production in 2000. Yet the statistics confirm experts' forecasts that very soon the North Sea will cease to be a significant player in the world's oil scenario.

LIKEWISE IN MEXICO

Mexico is another important non-OPEC country. Mexico and Norway were decisive in the oil price increases in 1999, when they joined with the OPEC countries and reduced production, thus strengthening the hand of OPEC in raising prices and keeping them high. Mexico is considered to have considerable potential reserves, especially in the Gulf of Mexico, but this area would require major investment to develop because of great depth of the water.

Furthermore, Mexico has already observed a decline in the number of wells in production, a situation that has been acknowledged by the General Director of the Mexican state oil company who noted that the "production has already begun to decline in some fields and there is a risk that oil exports will go down."[28] To turn this situation around will be very costly, but it is possible that the pressure could be restored in some of the oilfields. But the General Director has also admitted that PEMEX has only made one important discovery in the last twenty years, a field far from the coast in 1999.[29]

Let us look now at how the oil situation in Mexico has evolved. In the 1940s, Mexican oil production had a sustained growth of 5.7%, as the table shows.

Table 69. Mexico. Crude Oil Production. 1940s.

Years	Production	% Change
	thousands of barrels/day	
1940	120	
1941	115	-4.2
1942	95	-17.4
1943	96	1.1
1944	104	8.3
1945	119	14.4
1946	134	12.6
1947	154	14.9
1948	160	3.9
1949	166	3.8
1950	198	19.3
	Average Growth of Production	
	5.7	

Source: *Oil Facts and Figures, 1971 Edition. American Petroleum Institute. Page 548.*

In the 1950s oil production still grew, if not as fast as in the 1940s. But the reserves grew very handsomely, as shown below.

---

28. Producción No-OPEP. Agenda Petrolera Internacional. Facultad de Ciencias Económicas y Sociales. Universidad Central de Venezuela, edition August-September 2001, page 4.
29. Ibid.

Table 70. Mexico. Crude Oil Production and Reserves. 1950s.

Years	Production	% Change	Reserves	% Change
	thousands of barrels/day		*millions of barrels*	
1950	198			
1951	211	6.6		
1952	211	0.0		
1953	198	-6.2		
1954	229	15.7	1,424	
1955	244	6.6	1,525	7.1
1956	248	1.6	1,725	13.1
1957	241	-2.8	1,750	1.4
1958	256	6.2	1,900	8.6
1959	264	3.1	2,500	31.6
1960	271	2.7	2,500	0.0
	Average Growth of Production		Average Growth of Reserves	
	3.3		10.3	

Sources: Oil Facts and Figures, 1971 Edition, American Petroleum Institute. Page 548. Oil and Gas Journal 1999. Energy Statistics Sourcebook. P. 150.

In the 1960s, production grew at a rate similar to that of the 1950s, but the reserves failed to keep pace. Production grew on average by 4.4%, while the reserves were growing only at 0.3%.

Table 71. Mexico. Crude Oil Production and Reserves. 1960s.

Years	Production	% Change	Reserves	% Change
	thousands of barrels/day		*millions of barrels*	
1960	271		2,500	
1961	292	7.7	2,250	-10.0
1962	306	4.8	2,500	11.1
1963	314	2.6	2,500	0.0
1964	316	0.6	2,500	0.0
1965	323	2.2	2,800	12.0
1966	331	2.5	2,500	-10.7
1967	364	10.0	2,500	0.0
	Average Growth of Production		Average Growth of Reserves	
	4.4		0.3	

Sources: Oil Facts and Figures, 1971 Edition. American Petroleum Institute. Page 548.
Oil and Gas Journal 1999. Energy Statistics Sourcebook. P. 153.

In the 1970s, Mexican oil production received a great impetus. Indeed, production was boosted more than four times over that of the previous decade. The reserves also expanded rapidly, 41.5% on the average during this decade. This time, the balance was in favor of the reserves.

Table 72. Mexico. Crude Oil Production and Reserves. 1970s.

Year	Production	% Change	Reserves	% Change
	thousands of barrels/day		millions of barrels	
1970	420		6,000	
1971	433	3.1	3,200	-46.7
1972	444	2.5	4,500	40.6
1973	471	6.1	2,800	-37.8
1974	557	18.3	3,600	28.6
1975	722	29.6	13,582	277.3
1976	804	11.4	9,500	-30.1
1977	996	23.9	7,000	-26.3
1978	1,206	21.1	14,000	100.0
1979	1,461	21.1	16,000	14.3
1980	1,935	32.4	31,250	95.3
	Average Growth of Production		Average Growth of Reserves	
	17.0		41.5	

Source: Oil and Gas Journal 1999. Energy Statistics Sourcebook.

In the 1980s, Mexican oil production returned to its historical trend with an average growth of 3.5%, a little flat compared to the previous decade. The reserves, on the other hand, were still growing faster than production. In 1988, Mexico hit a "high-water mark" with 54.110 billion barrels of reserves. The vast increase in reserves registered during this decade is partly due to the inclusion of gas reserves in the statistics.

Table 73. Mexico. Crude Oil Production, Reserves and Consumption of Refined Products. 1980s.

Years	Production	% Change	Reserves	% Change	Consumption	% Change
	thousands of barrels/day		*millions of barrels*		*thousands of barrels/day*	
1980	1,935		31,250			
1981	2,312	19.5	48,084	53.9	1,311	—
1982	2,746	18.8	48,084	0.0	1,412	7.7
1983	2,665	-2.9	49,911	3.8	1,312	-7.1
1984	2,750	3.2	48,600	-2.6	1,270	-3.2
1985	2,703	-1.7	48,600	0.0	1,299	2.3
1986	2,427	-10.2	48,000	-1.2	1,348	3.8
1987	2,616	7.8	47,000	-2.1	1,415	5.0
1988	2,582	-1.3	54,110	15.1	1,460	3.2
1989	2,517	-2.5	51,983	-3.9	1,562	7.0
1990	2,639	4.8	51,298	-1.3	1,677	7.4
	Average Growth of Production		Average Growth of Reserves		Average Growth of Consumption	
	3.5		6.2		2.9	

Sources: OPEC Annual Statistical Bulletin 1982. Oil and Gas Journal 1999. Energy Statistics Sourcebook.

In the 1990s, Mexican oil production growth dropped below its historical trend to an average of 1.4%. However, 1998 saw the highest level of production ever experienced in this country. But even more important is the level of reserves, which declined to 28,300 million barrels for 2000, after having reached a maximum of 54,110 million barrels in 1988. This meant that Mexico in 2000 had only half the reserves it held in 1988, a pretty stark statistic.

The leaders of PEMEX have attributed this to the lack of investment in exploration due to the restrictions the country has been suffering since the payments crisis of 1982.

It should also be noted that the consumption of oil derivatives has grown considerably in Mexico, from 1.3 million barrels/day in 1981 to 2 million barrels/day in 2000. The Energy Information Administration of the United States Department of Energy sees Mexico as one of the countries that will most increase its domestic consumption of oil, which should double between 1997 and 2020.

Table 74. Mexico. Crude Oil: Production, Reserves and Consumption of Refined Products. 1990s.

Years	Production	% Change	Reserves	% Change	Consumption	% Change
	thousands of barrels/day		*millions of barrels*		*thousands of barrels/day*	
1990	2,639		51,298		1,677	
1991	2,675	1.4	50,925	-0.7	1,808	7.8
1992	2,667	-0.3	51,225	0.6	1,798	-0.6
1993	2,673	0.2	50,776	-0.9	1,810	0.7
1994	2,685	0.4	49,775	-2.0	1,900	5.0
1995	2,617	-2.5	48,796	-2.0	1,801	-5.2
1996	2,858	9.2	48,472	-0.7	1,885	4.7
1997	3,022	5.7	47,822	-1.3	1,947	3.3
1998	3,070	1.6	47,822	0.0	1,977	1.5
1999	2,906	-5.3	28,399	-40.6	2,028	2.6
2000	3,012	3.6	28,260	-0.5	2,067	1.9
	Average Growth of Production		Average Growth of Reserves		Average Growth of Consumption	
	1.4		-4.8		2.2	

Source: OPEC Annual Statistical Bulletin 1982; 1990; 1995; 2000.

Figure 12

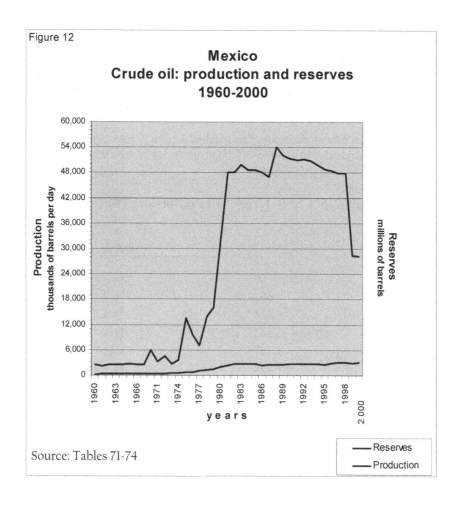

Mexico
Crude oil: production and reserves
1960-2000

Source: Tables 71-74

RUSSIA AND THE FORMER SOVIET UNION

The other great non-OPEC oil producer is Russia (and the countries of the former Soviet Union). Traditionally, these nations held their cards close to their chests, and data on strategic resources like oil were no exception. The statistics on oil production in the former Soviet Union are partial and there are gaps of several years.

In the 1940s, Soviet oil production reached a growth rate averaging 4.5%, from 609,000 barrels/day in 1940 to 748,000 barrels/day in the 1950s.

Table 75. USSR. Crude Oil Production. 1940.

Years	Production	% Change
	thousands of barrels/day	
1940	609	
1941	663	8.9
1942	634	-4.4
1943	563	-11.2
1944	767	36.2
1945	424	-44.7
1946	448	5.7
1947	532	18.8
1948	616	15.8
1949	670	8.8
1950	748	11.6
	Average Growth of Production	
	4.5	

Source: *Oil Facts and Figures, 1971 Edition, American Petroleum Institute. Page 550.*

The 1950s reconstruction period following the War — and the Cold War — drove Soviet oil production up from 748,000 barrels/day in 1950 to 2.2 million barrels/day in 1958. From that year, when the Soviet-Chinese bloc broke apart, to 1970, there are no statistics available.

Table 76. USSR. Crude Oil Production. 1950.

Years	Production	% Change
	thousands of barrels/day	
1950	748	
1951	800	7.0
1952	933	16.6
1953	1,041	11.6
1954	1,169	12.3
1955	1,396	19.4
1956	1,676	20.1
1957	1,966	17.3
1958	2,285	16.2
Average		15.1

Note: There is not available information on reserves. Source: Oil Facts and Figures, 1971 edition, American Petroleum Institute. Page 550.

In the 1970s, Soviet oil production registered an average growth rate of 5.5%, from 7 million barrels/day in 1970 up to 12 million barrels/day in 1980.

Table 77. USSR. Crude Oil Production. 1970s.

Years	Production	% Change
	thousands of barrels/day	
1970	7,048	
1971	7,435	5.5
1972	7,85	5.6
1973	8,417	7.2
1974	9,164	8.9
1975	9,823	7.2
1976	10,359	5.5
1977	10,926	5.5
1978	11,416	4.5
1979	11,706	2.5
1980	12,030	2.8
	Average Growth of Production 5.5	

Source: Oil and Gas Journal 1999. Energy Statistics Sourcebook. Page 102.

In the 1980s the production, the reserves and the consumption of the Soviet Union reached the highest levels in their history. In 1987, for example, it registered the highest production index, 12.4 million barrels/day. The reserves reached 86,054 million barrels in 1982. In 1989 the breakup of the Soviet Union took place.

Table 78. Former Soviet Union. Crude Oil Production, Reserves and Consumption of Refined Products. 1980s.

Years	Production	% Change	Reserves	% Change	Consumption	% Change
	thousands of barrels/ day		*millions of barrels*		*thousands of barrels/day*	
1980	12,030		63,000			
1981	12,176	1.2	85,000	34.9	8,971	—
1982	12,251	0.6	86,054	1.2	9,003	0.4
1983	12,325	0.6	84,846	-1.4	8,974	-0.3
1984	12,279	-0.4	81,000	-4.5	8,830	-1.6
1985	11,882	-3.2	75,000	-7.4	—	—
1986	12,289	3.4	60,700	-19.1	8,899	—
1987	12,483	1.6	59,000	-2.8	8,901	0.0
1988	12,452	-0.2	58,500	-0.8	8,777	-1.4
1989	12,300	-1.2	58,400	-0.2	8,658	-1.4
1990	11,550	-6.1	57,000	-2.4	8,052	-7.0
	Average Growth of Production		Average Growth of Reserves		Average Growth of Consumption	
	-0.4		-0.2		-1.6	

Source: OPEC Annual Statistical Bulletin 1982; 1984; 1985; 1989; 1990.

Production declined in the 1990s. The breakup of the Soviet Union and the attendant economic crisis were reflected directly in the oil production results.

The reserves were also stagnated at 57 billion barrels between 1990 and 1995. The reserves grew to 65 billion barrels in 1996, but dropped back to 63 billion barrels in 2000. That is to say that reserves remained roughly stagnant in the vicinity of 65 billion barrels or less during the last years of the decade. Why is that? Either way, one thing is certain: in Russia and the former Soviet Union, reserves failed to grow in the last decade of the 20th century and this introduced an element of doubt as to this country's ability to increase its future oil inventories. Their reserves in 2000 were 63.5 billion barrels, while their highest level was 86 billion in 1982. This is a drastic reduction and is a dire sign for the future.

Table 79. Former Soviet Union. Crude Oil: Production, Reserves and Consumption of Refined Products. 1990s.

Years	Production	% Change	Reserves	% Change	Consump- tion	% Change
	thousands of barrels/ day		*millions of barrels*		*thousands of barrels/day*	
1990	11,550		57,000		8,052	
1991	10,367	-10.2	57,000	0.0	8,300	3.1
1992	8,995	-13.2	57,000	0.0	6,622	-20.2
1993	7,813	-13.1	57,000	0.0	5,490	-17.1
1994	7,045	-9.8	57,000	0.0	4,671	-14.9
1995	7,059	0.2	57,000	0.0	4,575	-2.1
1996	7,034	-0.4	65,405	14.7	4,244	-7.2
1997	7,214	2.6	65,405	0.0	4,343	2.3
1998	7,242	0.4	65,405	0.0	4,199	-3.3
1999	7,434	2.7	65,405	0.0	3,995	-4.9
2000	7,459	0.3	63,505	-2.9	3,765	-5.8
	Average Growth of Production		Average Growth of Reserves		Average Growth of Consumption	
	-4.1		1.2		-7.0	

Source: OPEC Annual Statistical Bulletin 1982; 1985; 1990; 1995; 1999; 2000.

Conclusion about Russia and the Former Soviet Union

The figures clearly show that until 2000, the heyday of oil production in the Soviet Union was in 1987, when it reached 12.4 million barrels/day. Then, production began to go down. Is that due to the political process of the breakup of the Soviet Union? Or is it due to a natural decline in its oil fields and the decrease of reserves? Is the situation permanent or is it only a temporary crisis? We can only wait and see what happens next.

THE CASPIAN SEA

With the Soviet Union disintegrated, the international oil companies gained the possibility of exploiting the resources of Caspian Sea. Great reserves of oil and gas are thought to exist in the region but no one can say precisely how much.

Rights to these resources are disputed. Several countries have direct coasts on the Caspian Sea. To the north are Russia and Kazakhstan, to the east, Turkmenistan, to the west Russia and Azerbaijan, and to the south, Iran. Moreover, the rest of the world has its eye on the region, too; and the United States in particular covets the oil there.

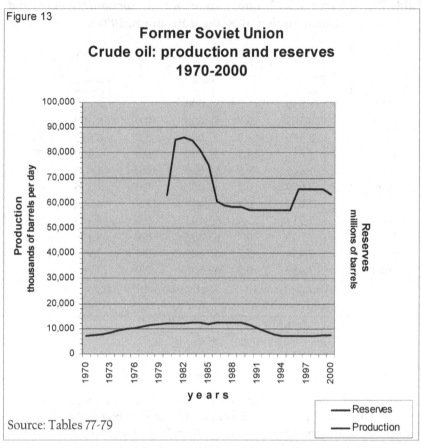

Figure 13

**Former Soviet Union
Crude oil: production and reserves
1970-2000**

Source: Tables 77-79

Furthermore, the juridical status has not been defined. International law makes different provisions depending on whether a body of water is defined as a sea or a lake. If it is accepted that it is a lake, then the neighboring countries would have to exploit the region in condominium. If it is accepted that it is a sea, each country could exploit it own coastline. Indeed, the Caspian is relatively small. It is far smaller than the Mediterranean and other seas.

Added to the problem of the legal definition of the area is the awkward logistical fact that the Caspian is a long way from anywhere. Enormous international pipelines will be required to get the oil out to the consumer market. The pipelines will have to cross countries that are or may soon be in conflict; one possible route would be across Iran, from north to south, to the Persian Gulf or the Gulf of Oman. But at any moment Iran could interrupt the oil supply for political reasons. The West would never feel that its oil supply through Iran was guaranteed. Another possible route would be to the west, crossing Azerbaijan and Georgia and arriving at Turkey's coast on the Mediterranean Sea. This would require political agreements with several countries. Another alternative would be to build a great pipeline toward the east, crossing Turkmenistan, Afghanistan and Pakistan, to the Arabian Sea.

THE STRATEGIC IMPORTANCE OF AFGHANISTAN

Any oil going from the Caspian Sea east towards the Arabian Sea has to pass through Afghanistan. Afghanistan's neighbors are oil countries. To the north it borders with the former Soviet republics of Turkmenistan, Uzbekistan and Tajikistan. To the west it borders on Iran. Just east of Afghanistan is the Tarim Region in northwest China, which is also thought to be a potential oil-producing region. Thus it seems possible that Afghanistan also has a great potential in hydrocarbons, that is to say that it forms part of the same energy basin.

Afghanistan becomes a political objective of the first order as soon as the oil resources of the Caspian Sea and its neighbors can be exploited.

CHINA

China is another non-OPEC country that has considerable potential reserves, particularly in the northwest, in the Tarim Region and in the south, in the South China Sea.

The Tarim Region borders on Kazakhstan, Tajikistan, Pakistan and India. Here, there is no territorial dispute. But in the South China Sea, the oil and gas reserves that are believed to exist around the Spratly Archipelago are the focus of a lively contest among all the neighboring countries, including Vietnam, Taiwan, the Philippines and Malaysia.

In the 1940s Chinese oil production was hardly 300 barrels/day. Just four years later, production was increased to 1,400 barrels/day and by 1950 it had already reached 2,200 barrels/day.

Table 80. China. Crude Oil Production. 1940s.

Years	Production	% Change
	thousands of barrels/day	
1940	0.3	
1941	0.2	-12.8
1942	0.9	291.2
1943	1.2	31.5
1944	1.4	13.0
1945	1.3	-4.1
1946	1.4	6.0
1947	1	-27.1
1948	1.5	42.6
1949	2	37.0
1950	2.2	9.6
Average Growth of production		
38.7		

Source: Oil Facts and Figures, 1971 Edition, American Petroleum Institute. Page 554.

In the 1950s, production grew modestly from 2,200 barrels/day in 1950 to 16,400 barrels/day in 1958. In that year the breakup of the Chinese-Soviet bloc meant, once again, that statistics are lacking until 1970.

Table 81. China. Crude Oil Production. 1950.

Years	Production	% Change
	thousands of barrels/day	
1950	2.2	
1951	2.5	12.5
1952	2.7	11.1
1953	4.1	50.0
1954	8.2	100.0
1955	9.6	16.7
1956	12.9	34.3
1957	13.7	6.4
1958	16.4	20.0
Average Growth of production		
31.4		

Source: Oil Facts and Figures, 1971 Edition, American Petroleum Institute. Page 554.

In 1970, production was only 210,000 barrels/day. But within five years, by 1975, China passed one million 400,000 barrels/day. In 1980, Chinese production was already at 2,177,000 barrels/day.

Table 82. China. Crude Oil Production. 1970s.

Years	Production	% Change
	thousands of barrels/day	
1970	210	
1971	326	55.2
1972	525	61.0
1973	645	22.9
1974	970	50.4
1975	1,450	49.5
1976	1,652	13.9
1977	1,780	7.7
1978	1,916	7.6
1979	2,129	11.1
1980	2,177	2.3
	Average Growth of Production	
	28.2	

Source: Oil and Gas Journal 1999. Energy Statistics Sourcebook. P. 103

In the 1980s, production grew at a moderate rate, from 2.1 million barrels/day in 1980 to 2.7 million barrels/day in 1990. For most of this decade the reserves stayed about the same, until an increase was recorded in the last three years.

Between 1980 and 1995, production remained stable between 2.0 and 2.9 million barrels/day. Starting in 1996 it surpassed 3 million barrels/day to reach its maximum historical level of 3,252,000 barrels/day in 1997. Then, it began a downturn. Thus, 1997 may have been China's year of peak production.

Table 83. China. Crude Oil Production, Reserves and Consumption of Refined Products. 1980s.

Years	Production	% Change	Reserves	% Change	Consumption	% Change
	thousands of barrels/day		*millions of barrels*		*thousands of barrels/day*	
1980	2,177		20,500			
1981	2,022	-7.1	18,500	-9.8	1,661	—
1982	2,040	0.9	18,200	-1.6	1,646	-0.9
1983	2,121	4.0	18,200	0.0	1,710	3.9
1984	2,194	3.4	18,200	0.0	1,730	1.2
1985	2,497	13.8	18,420	1.2	—	—
1986	2,620	4.9	18,400	-0.1	1,930	—
1987	2,687	2.6	18,400	0.0	2,056	6.5
1988	2,740	2.0	23,550	28.0	2,124	3.3
1989	2,842	3.7	24,000	1.9	2,211	4.1
1990	2,767	-2.6	24,000	0.0	2,189	-1.0
	Average Growth of Production		Average Growth of Reserves		Average Growth of Consumption	
	2.6		2.0		2.4	

Source: OPEC Annual Statistical Bulletin 1982; 1984; 1985; 1989; 1990; 1995; 1999.

Table 84. China. Crude Oil Production, Reserves and Consumption of Refined Products. 1990s.

Years	Production	% Change	Reserves	% Change	Consumption	% Change
	thousands of barrels/day		*millions of barrels*		*thousands of barrels/day*	
1990	2,767		24,000		2,189	
1991	2,804	1.3	24,000	0.0	2,427	10.9
1992	2,814	0.4	24,000	0.0	2,625	8.2
1993	2,910	3.4	24,000	0.0	2,882	9.8
1994	2,974	2.2	24,000	0.0	3,031	5.2
1995	2,996	0.7	24,000	0.0	3,218	6.2
1996	3,173	5.9	24,000	0.0	3,539	10.0
1997	3,252	2.5	24,000	0.0	3,963	12.0
1998	3,215	-1.1	24,000	0.0	3,839	-3.1
1999	3,211	-0.1	24,000	0.0	4,169	8.6
2000	3,228	0.5	24,000	0.0	4,675	12.1
	Average Growth of Production		Average Growth of Reserves		Average Growth of Consumption	
	1.6		0.0		8.0	

Source: OPEC Annual Statistical Bulletin 1990; 1995; 1999; 2000.

CHINESE RESERVES ARE RUNNING OUT

From 1989 to 2000, China did not manage to increase the size of its reserves. This is evidence that China's oil supply is being drained down and that new reserves are not being discovered, or not in sufficient quantity.

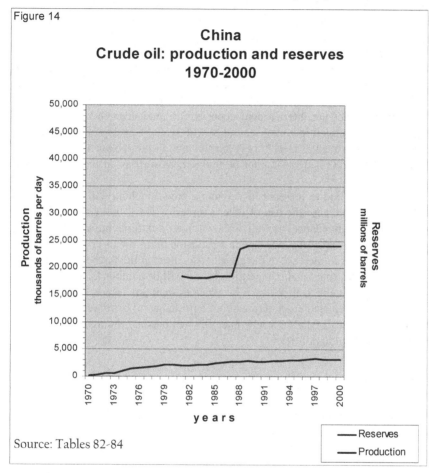

Figure 14

**China
Crude oil: production and reserves
1970-2000**

Source: Tables 82-84

CHINA'S FUTURE CONSUMPTION

Consumption projections for China in the first twenty years of the current century suggest an enormous appetite for oil, more than 2.5 times its current consumption. If China is not able to discover more oil in its potentially rich oilfields, that alone will cause a crunch of massive proportions.

China is looking for oil outside of its own territory and its area of influence. For example, it has agreements with Venezuela. If China had enough oil in its own area, the logical plan would be to concentrate on the exploration and exploitation of those areas, and not to go around the world in search of oil. Consequently, it can be inferred that such potential either does not exist or that its true capacity is in doubt. China's oil potential will be known only when its probable and possible reserves in the Tarim Region and in the South China See become proven reserves. Only then can we speak with certainty about the extent of the Chinese reserves. Meanwhile, they are only hypothetical.

China is the emerging power in the new millennium. Just as in the 1950s China fought to be accepted in the United Nations and later to become a member of the Security Council, now has entered the World Trade Organization, a fact that would impact the international economic relationships, because it would generate new competition in prices at world scale. Developed countries see China as a vast potential market (any surplus purchasing power in a country of well over a billion residents cannot be ignored) as well as an unbeatable competitor as a producer.

To maintain and to increase its economic growth, China will need more oil and will surely increase the use of other sources of fossil fuel energy, like coal (which it has an abundance) as well. This will have a definite impact on the environment. Consequently, it is a foregone conclusion that China's economic growth will contribute to an increase in the greenhouse effect in the foreseeable future.

The statistics show that competition for oil will be a major factor in the fight for each country's survival. When it becomes evident how scarce oil is, and that its reserves are depleted every day without any chance of being recovered, international politics will take on a new hue. Oil will become the main objective of diplomacy and world politics.

CONCLUSION ABOUT THE NON-OPEC COUNTRIES

The United States has seen its reserves decline drastically since the 1970s. And the trend seems only to get worse.

The United Kingdom managed to expand its reserves moderately during the 1990s, while Norway and Mexico lost ground. According to public statistics, the Soviet Union held its own in terms of oil reserves, as did China. It can be concluded then that the non-OPEC countries are facing a clear decrease in their oil reserves. If the reserves are running out or fail to grow, we clearly will not have long to wait before a great oil crisis erupts. But that will be a crisis completely different from those that we have seen up to now, because this time it will be the consequence of an actual lack of oil and not of political decisions.

CHAPTER 10. CRUDE OIL IN THE OPEC COUNTRIES

THE PRODUCTION PEAK IN THE MIDDLE EAST

By 1997, most of the non-OPEC countries had already reached their maximum levels of production, so that we can assume that the process of exhaustion of reserves outside of OPEC has already begun, according to the Hubbert Curve. But the OPEC countries are confronting the same situation as the non-OPEC countries.

Some countries in the Middle East have already arrived at their maximum levels of production and their decline can be predicted to begin. Experts have affirmed that the point when oil will enter a decline worldwide would begin in 2005, that is, 2005 is the year when the decline should begin in most of the OPEC countries. Let us now look at them one by one.

In the 1960s, production grew about four times faster than reserves.

Table 85. Algeria. Crude Oil Production and Reserves. 1960s.

Years	Production	% Change	Reserves	% Change
	thousands of barrels/day		*millions of barrels*	
1960	181		5,000	
1961	330	82.3	5,200	4.0
1962	436	32.1	5,500	5.8
1963	504	15.6	6,500	18.2
1964	557	10.5	7,000	7.7
1965	558	0.2	7,500	7.1
1966	718	28.7	7,400	-1.3
1967	825	14.9	7,250	-2.0
1968	904	9.6	6,900	-4.8
1969	946	4.6	7,000	1.4
1970	1,029	8.8	8,000	14.3
	Average Growth of Production		Average Growth of Reserves	
	20.7		5.0	

Sources: OPEC Annual Statistical Bulletin 1990.
Oil and Gas Journal 1999. Energy Statistics Sourcebook.

ALGERIA IN THE 1970S

In the 1970s the reserves grew significantly. It began at 8 billion of barrels and in the next 3 years it almost multiplied by six to arrive to 47 billion of barrels. But it fell again and the decade closed with a level of 8.4 billion barrels. In 1978 Algeria reached their maximum production levels. Starting from then the reserves began to decline, just as it can be observed in the following tables. In this decade Algeria also had its highest level of reserves, 47 billion barrels in 1973 that also began to descend to arrive in 2000 to only 11,300 million barrels, facts that put in evidence the oil exhaustion in this country.

Table 86. Algeria. Crude Oil Production and Reserves. 1970s.

Years	Production	% Change	Reserves	% Change
	thousands of barrels/day		*millions of barrels*	
1970	1,029		8,000	
1971	785	-23.7	30,000	275.0
1972	1,062	35.3	12,250	-59.2
1973	1,097	3.3	47,000	-61.6
1974	1,008	-8.1	7,640	62.6
1975	982	-2.6	7,700	0.8
1976	1,075	9.5	7,370	-4.3
1977	1,152	7.2	6,800	-7.7
1978	1,161	0.8	6,600	-2.9
1979	1,153	-0.7	6,300	-4.5
1980	1,019	-11.6	8,400	33.3
	Average Growth of Production		Average Growth of Reserves	
	0.9		23.1	

Sources: OPEC Annual Statistical Bulletin 1990.
Oil and Gas Journal 1999. Energy Statistics Sourcebook.

ALGERIA IN THE 1980S

In the 1980s the reserves grew modestly and production fell. This is consistent with trends worldwide in those years.

Table 87. Algeria. Crude Oil Production, Reserves and Consumption of Refined Products. 1980s.

Years	Production	% Change	Reserves	% Change	Consumption	% Change
	thousands of barrels/ day		*millions of barrels*		*thousands of barrels/day*	
1980	1,019		8,200			
1981	797	-21.8	8,080	-1.5	111	—
1982	704	-11.7	9,440	16.8	123	10.8
1983	660	-6.3	9,220	-2.3	128	4.1
1984	695	5.3	9,000	-2.4	140	9.4
1985	672	-3.3	8,820	-2.0	148	5.7
1986	673	0.1	8,800	-0.2	147	-0.7
1987	648	-3.7	8,500	-3.4	152	3.4
1988	650	0.3	9,200	8.2	158	3.9
1989	727	11.8	9,236	0.4	168	6.3
1990	788	8.4	9,200	-0.4	187	11.3
	Average Growth of Production		Average Growth of Reserves		Average Growth of Consumption	
	-2.1		1.3		6.0	

Sources: OPEC Annual Statistical Bulletin 1984; 1985, 1989; 1990. Sources: OPEC Annual Statistical Bulletin 1984; 1985, 1989; 1990.

ALGERIA IN THE 1990S

In the 1990s, the situation changed. The reserves grew at 2.1% on average, surpassing the growth rate for production (which was minimal in this period).

Table 88. Algeria. Crude Oil Production, Reserves and Consumption of Refined Products. 1990s.

Years	Production	% Change	Reserves	% Change	Consump-tion	% Change
	thousands of barrels/day		*millions of barrels*		*thousands of barrels/day*	
1990	788		9,200		187	
1991	803	1.9	9,200	0.0	162	-13.4
1992	756	-5.9	9,200	0.0	190	17.3
1993	747	-1.2	9,200	0.0	186	-2.1
1994	752	0.7	9,979	8.5	177	-4.8
1995	752	0.0	9,979	0.0	172	-2.8
1996	805	7.0	10,800	8.2	168	-2.3
1997	846	5.1	11,200	3.7	163	-3.0
1998	827	-2.2	11,314	1.0	171	4.9
1999	749	-9.4	11,314	0.0	185	8.2
2000	796	6.3	11,314	0.0	—	—
	Average Growth of Production		Average Growth of Reserves		Average Growth of Consumption	
	0.2		2.1		0.2	

Source: OPEC Annual Statistical Bulletin1985, 1990, 1995; 1999; 2000.

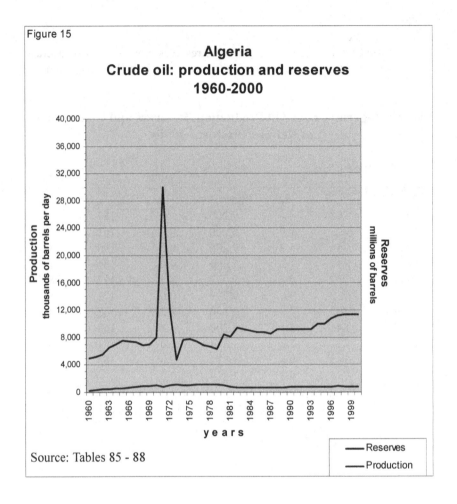

Figure 15

**Algeria
Crude oil: production and reserves
1960-2000**

Source: Tables 85 - 88

INDONESIA IN THE 1960S

Practically speaking, Indonesia's reserves did not grow in the 1960s. On the other hand, production increased significantly. In other words, there was a net reduction of the reserves.

Table 89. Indonesia. Crude Oil Production and Reserves. 1960s.

Years	Production	% Change	Reserves	% Change
	thousands of barrels/day		*millions of barrels*	
1960	409		9,000	
1961	424	3.7	9,500	5.6
1962	453	6.8	9,500	0.0
1963	444	-2.0	10,000	5.3
1964	456	2.7	10,000	0.0
1965	480	5.3	10,000	0.0
1966	464	-3.3	9,500	-5.0
1967	505	8.8	9,100	-4.2
1968	600	18.8	9,000	-1.1
1969	742	23.7	8,850	-1.7
1970	853	15.0	9,000	1.7
	Average Growth of Production		Average Growth of Reserves	
	7.9		0.1	

Sources: OPEC Annual Statistical Bulletin 1990. Oil and Gas Journal 1999. Energy Statistics Sourcebook.

Production growth in the 1970s was triple the reserves growth rate. In 1977, Indonesia had the greatest production in the last forty years. Since then, production generally fell. In this decade Indonesia also reached its highest level of reserves, 15 billion barrels, in 1975.

Table 90. Indonesia. Crude Oil Production and Reserves. 1970s.

Years	Production	% Change	Reserves	% Change
	thousands of barrels/day		*millions of barrels*	
1970	853		9,000	
1971	892	4.6	10,000	11.1
1972	1,080	21.1	10,400	4.0
1973	1,338	23.9	10,005	-3.8
1974	1,374	2.7	10,500	4.9
1975	1,306	-4.9	15,000	42.9
1976	1,503	15.1	14,000	-6.7
1977	1,686	12.2	10,500	-25.0
1978	1,635	-3.0	10,000	-4.8
1979	1,590	-2.8	10,200	2.0
1980	1,575	-0.9	9,600	-5.9
	Average Growth of Production		Average Growth of Reserves	
	6.8		1.9	

Sources: OPEC Annual Statistical Bulletin 1990;Oil and Gas Journal 1999. Energy Statistics Sourcebook.

Following the global trend, Indonesia's reserves are reported to have grown faster than production in the 1980s.

Table 91. Indonesia. Crude Oil Production, Reserves and Consumption of Refined Products. 1980s.

Years	Production	% Change	Reserves	% Change	Consumption	% Change
	thousands of barrels/ day		*millions of barrels*		*thousands of barrels/ day*	
1980	1,575		9,600			
1981	1,604	1.8	9,800	2.1	458	
1982	1,324	-17.5	9,550	-2.6	479	-4.5
1983	1,245	-6.0	9,100	-4.7	467	-2.5
1984	1,280	2.8	8,650	-4.9	468	0.2
1985	1,181	-7.7	8,500	-1.7	464	0.8
1986	1,256	6.4	9,000	5.9	470	1.3
1987	1,158	-7.8	9,000	0.0	491	4.5
1988	1,177	1.6	9,000	0.0	514	4.7
1989	1,231	4.6	11,050	22.8	547	6.4
1990	1,280	4.0	11,050	0.0	629	15.0
	Average Growth of Production		Average Growth of Reserves		Average Growth of Consumption	
	-1.8		1.7		3.7	

Source: OPEC Annual Statistical Bulletin 1984; 1989; 1990.

INDONESIA IN THE 1990S

The reserves shrank significantly in the following decade. On the whole, in the forty years covered by this analysis, the tendency of reserves to start to diminish while production was still increasing is clear. This simply means that the reserves were being depleted.

Table 92. Indonesia. Crude Oil Production, Reserves and Consumption of Refined Products.

Years	Production	% Change	Reserves	% Change	Consumption	% Change
	thousands of barrels/day		millions of barrels		thousands of barrels/day	
1990	1,280		11,050		629	
1991	1,450	13.3	10,247	-7.3	661	5.1
1992	1,347	-7.1	5,597	-45.4	701	6.1
1993	1,327	-1.5	5,128	-8.4	711	1.4
1994	1,332	0.4	5,128	0.0	751	5.6
1995	1,328	-0.3	4,979	-2.9	774	3.1
1996	1,326	-0.2	4,979	0.0	865	11.8
1997	1,330	0.3	4,979	0.0	946	9.4
1998	1,315	-1.1	4,979	0.0	896	-5.3
1999	1,207	-8.2	5,200	4.4	846	-5.6
2000	1,272	5.4	5,100	-1.9	1,034	22.2
	Average Growth of Production		Average Growth of Reserves		Average Growth of Consumption	
	0.1		-6.1		5.4	

Source: OPEC Annual Statistical Bulletin 1990; 1995; 1999; 2000.

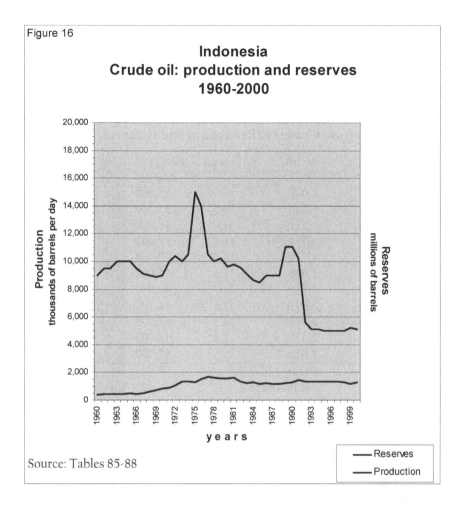

Figure 16

Indonesia
Crude oil: production and reserves
1960-2000

Source: Tables 85-88

Iran's oil production in the 1960s grew almost three times faster than the reserves. In other words, the speed at which oil was pumped out was far greater than the speed at which new reserves were found and confirmed.

Table 93. Iran. Crude Oil Production and Reserves. 1960s.

Years	Production	% Change	Reserves	% Change
	thousands of barrels/day		*millions of barrels*	
1960	1,098		35,000	
1961	1,202	9.5	35,000	0.0
1962	1,334	11.0	35,000	0.0
1963	1,491	11.8	37,000	5.7
1964	1,710	14.7	37,000	0.0
1965	1,908	11.6	38,000	2.7
1966	2,131	11.7	40,000	5.3
1967	2,603	22.1	44,200	10.5
1968	2,971	14.1	43,800	-0.9
1969	3,375	13.6	54,000	23.3
1970	3,829	13.5	55,000	1.9
	Average Growth of Production		Average Growth of Reserves	
	13.4		4.8	

Sources: OPEC Annual Statistical Bulletin 1990. Oil and Gas Journal 1999. Energy Statistics Sourcebook.

IRAN IN THE 1970S

In the 1970s — for the first time — Iran's reserves grew faster than production, production having dropped by more than half between 1970 and 1980. In 1974 Iran reached its maximum level of production. In the following years it decreased significantly.

Table 94. Iran. Crude Oil Production and Reserves. 1970s.

Years	Production	% Change	Reserves	% Change
	thousands of barrels/day		*millions of barrels*	
1970	3,829		55,000	
1971	4,539	18.5	70,000	27.3
1972	5,023	10.7	55,500	-20.7
1973	5,860	16.7	65,000	17.1
1974	6,021	2.7	60,000	-7.7
1975	5,350	-11.1	66,000	10.0
1976	5,882	9.9	64,500	-2.3
1977	5,662	-3.7	63,000	-2.3
1978	5,241	-7.4	62,000	-1.6
1979	3,167	-39.6	59,000	-4.8
1980	1,467	-53.7	58,000	-1.7
	Average Growth of Production		Average Growth of Reserves	
	-5.7		1.3	

Sources: OPEC Annual Statistical Bulletin 1984. Oil and Gas Journal 1999. Energy Statistics Sourcebook.

IRAN IN THE 1980S

The highest level of production Iran reached in the 1980s was 3.1 million barrels/day, a figure that contrasts with its maximum production: 6 million barrels/day, achieved in 1974. The havoc caused by the Iran–Iraq war, which was drawn out for eight years between 1980 and 1988, kept down production and the reserves remained static between 1986 and 1990.

Table 95. Iran. Crude Oil Production, Reserves and Consumption of Refined Products. 1980s.

Years	Production	% Change	Reserves	% Change	Consump-tion	% Change
	thousands of barrels/ day		*millions of barrels*		*thousands of barrels/day*	
1980	1,467		58,000			
1981	1,315	-10.4	57,000	-1.7	618	—
1982	2,391	81.8	55,308	-3.0	719	16.3
1983	2,441	2.1	51,000	-7.8	871	21.1
1984	2,032	-16.8	58,874	15.4	723	-17.0
1985	2,192	7.9	59,000	0.2	735	1.7
1986	2,037	-7.1	92,860	57.4	711	-3.3
1987	2,297	12.8	92,860	0.0	751	5.6
1988	2,305	0.3	92,860	0.0	766	2.0
1989	2,814	22.1	92,860	0.0	778	1.6
1990	3,182	13.1	92,850	0.0	850	9.3
	Average Growth of Production		Average Growth of Reserves		Average Growth of Consumption	
	10.6		6.1		4.1	

Source: OPEC Annual Statistical Bulletin 1983; 1984; 1985; 1989; 1990.

IRAN IN THE 1990S

After the war against Iraq was ended, Iran's reserves stayed about the same, as did production. This would appear to confirm that oil was becoming harder to find in Iran, one of the world's largest producers.

Table 96. Iran. Crude Oil Production, Reserves and Consumption of Refined Products. 1990s.

Years	Production	% Change	Reserves	% Change	Consump-tion	% Change
	thousands of barrels/day		*millions of barrels*		*thousands of barrels/day*	
1990	3,182		92,850		850	
1991	3,407	7.1	92,860	0.0	892	4.9
1992	3,431	0.7	92,860	0.0	940	5.4
1993	3,425	-0.2	92,860	0.0	960	2.1
1994	3,596	5.0	94,300	1.6	920	-4.2
1995	3,595	0.0	93,700	-0.6	945	2.7
1996	3,596	0.0	92,600	-1.2	984	4.1
1997	3,603	0.2	92,600	0.0	981	-0.3
1998	3,714	3.1	93,700	1.2	1,318	34.4
1999	3,439	-7.4	93,100	-0.6	1,192	-9.6
	Average Growth of Production		Average Growth of Reserves		Average Growth of Consumption	
	0.9		0.0		4.4	

Source: OPEC Annual Statistical Bulletin 1995; 1999; 2000.

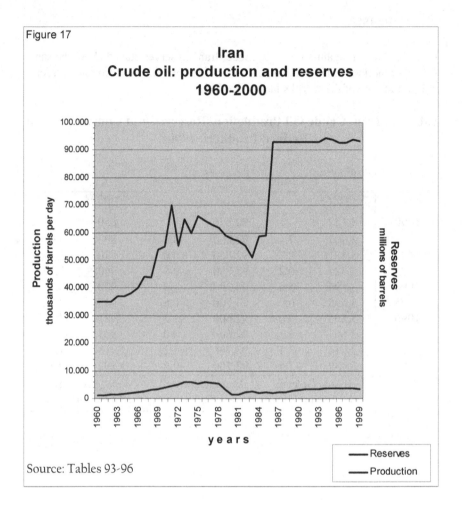

Figure 17

**Iran
Crude oil: production and reserves
1960-2000**

Source: Tables 93-96

IRAQ IN THE 1960S

In this 1960s, the average production growth of Iraq was five times the reserves growth rate.

Table 97. Iraq. Crude Oil Production and Reserves. 1960s.

Years	Production	% Change	Reserves	% Change
	thousands of barrels/day		*millions of barrels*	
1960	972		25,000	
1961	1,007	3.6	27,000	8.0
1962	1,009	0.2	26,500	-1.9
1963	1,161	15.1	26,000	-1.9
1964	1,252	7.8	25,500	-1.9
1965	1,312	4.8	25,000	-2.0
1966	1,392	6.1	25,000	0.0
1967	1,228	-11.8	24,000	-4.0
1968	1,503	22.4	23,500	-2.1
1969	1,521	1.2	28,000	19.1
1970	1,548	1.8	27,500	-1.8
	Average Growth of Production		Average Growth of Reserves	
	5.1		1.2	

Sources: OPEC Annual Statistical Bulletin 1990. Oil and Gas Journal 1999. Energy Statistics Sourcebook.

IRAQ IN THE 1970S

In the 1970s, as in 1960s, production went up faster than the reserves; seven times faster, in this case.

In 1979, Iraq reached its highest production level in forty years. However, this figure does not completely reflect reality, since in the 1990s Iraq was sanctioned by the United Nations and was only allowed to export a very limited quantity of oil, and its production capacity was limited by this circumstance. But, up to now, production figures for 1979 are is an important reference mark when we consider the possible beginning of the oil decline of this country.

Table 98. Iraq. Crude Oil Production and Reserves. 1970s.

Years	Production	% Change	Reserves	% Change
	thousands of barrels/day		*millions of barrels*	
1970	1,548		27,500	
1971	1,694	9.4	32,000	16.4
1972	1,465	-13.5	35,990	12.5
1973	2,018	37.7	29,000	-19.4
1974	1,970	-2.4	31,500	8.6
1975	2,261	14.8	35,000	11.1
1976	2,415	6.8	34,300	-2.0
1977	2,348	-2.8	34,000	-0.9
1978	2,562	9.1	34,500	1.5
1979	3,476	35.7	32,100	-7.0
1980	2,646	-23.9	31,000	-3.4
	Average Growth of Production		Average Growth of Reserves	
	7.1		1.7	

Sources: OPEC, Annual Statistical Bulletin 1984. Oil and Gas Journal 1999. Energy Statistics Sourcebook.

IRAQ IN THE 1980s

In the 1980s the situation was different. For first time the average growth of the reserves surpassed by a considerable margin the average growth of production, as it did elsewhere during that decade.

Table 99. Iraq. Crude Oil Production, Reserves and Consumption of Refined Products. 1980s.

Years	Production	% Change	Reserves	% Change	Consumption	% Change
	thousands of barrels/ day		*millions of barrels*		*thousands of barrels/day*	
1980	2,646		30,000			
1981	897	-66.1	29,700	-1.0	204	—
1982	1,012	12.8	59,000	98.7	203	-0.5
1983	1,098	8.5	65,000	10.2	249	22.7
1984	1,221	11.2	65,000	0.0	234	-6.0
1985	1,404	15.0	65,000	0.0	285	21.8
1986	1,876	33.6	72,000	10.8	261	-8.4
1987	2,358	25.7	100,000	38.9	281	7.7
1988	2,739	16.2	100,000	0.0	294	4.6
1989	2,785	1.7	100,000	0.0	303	3.1
1990	2,125	-23.7	100,000	0.0	325	7.3
	Average Growth of Production		Average Growth of Reserves		Average Growth of Consumption	
	3.5		15.7		5.8	

Source: OPEC Annual Statistical Bulletin 1982; 1984; 1985; 1989; 1990; 1995; 1999.

In the 1990s a completely contrary phenomenon was seen. The average production growth was 21.1%, while the reserves growth was hardly 1.2% on average, which is close to stagnation. Indeed, Iraq's reserves hovered around 112.5 billion barrels from 1996 until 2000, and that is the highest reserves figure reached by Iraq to date. As a consequence of the invasion of Kuwait, in these years Iraq was subjected to international sanctions that limited its oil production. Was this the only circumstance that kept Iraq from expanding its reserves, or does Iraq simply not have more oil in its territory?

Table 100. Iraq. Crude Oil Production, Reserves and Consumption of Refined Products. 1990s.

Years	Production	% Change	Reserves	% Change	Consumption	% Change
	thousands of barrels/day		*millions of barrels*		*thousands of barrels/day*	
1990	2,125		100,000		325	
1991	277	-87.0	100,000	0.0	308	-5.2
1992	526	89.9	100,000	0.0	440	42.9
1993	659	25.3	100,000	0.0	563	28.0
1994	748	13.5	100,000	0.0	623	10.7
1995	736	-1.6	100,000	0.0	612	-1.8
1996	740	0.5	112,000	12.0	594	-2.9
1997	1,383	86.9	112,500	0.4	601	1.2
1998	2,181	57.7	112,500	0.0	620	3.2
1999	2,719	24.7	112,500	0.0	599	-3.4
2000	2,810	3.3	112,500	0.0	655	9.3
	Average Growth of Production		Average Growth of Reserves		Average Growth of Consumption	
	21.3		1.2		8.2	

Source: OPEC Annual Statistical Bulletin 1990; 1995; 1999; 2000.

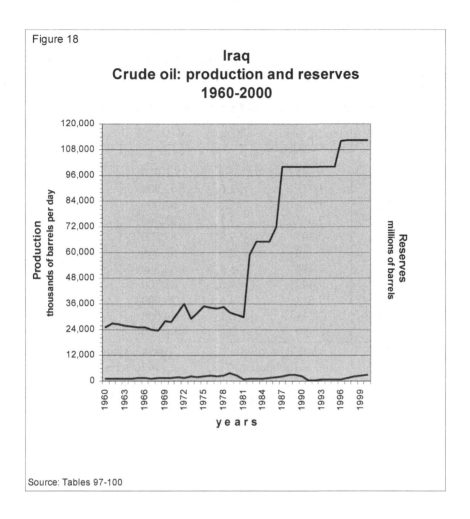

Figure 18

Iraq
Crude oil: production and reserves
1960-2000

Source: Tables 97-100

KUWAIT IN THE 1960S

Between 1960 and 1970 the reserves grew modestly, only one per cent on average, while production grew faster, as can be seen in the table.

Table 101. Kuwait. Crude Oil Production and Reserves. 1960s.

Years	Production	% Change	Reserves	% Change
	thousands of barrels/ day		*millions of barrels*	
1960	1,691	—	62,000	—
1961	1,735	2.6	62,000	0.0
1962	1,957	12.8	62,000	0.0
1963	2,096	7.1	63,000	1.6
1964	2,301	9.8	63,500	0.8
1965	2,360	2.6	63,000	-0.8
1966	2,484	5.3	62,500	-0.8
1967	2,499	0.6	68,700	9.9
1968	2,613	4.6	70,000	1.9
1969	2,773	6.1	69,000	-1.4
1970	2,989	7.8	68,000	-1.4
	Average Growth of Production		Average Growth of Reserves	
	5.9		1.0	

Sources: OPEC Annual Statistical Bulletin 1990.
Oil and Gas Journal 1999. Energy Statistics Sourcebook.

KUWAIT IN THE 1970S

In this period the reserves diminished. Production also diminished. Kuwait's highest rate of oil production in the last forty years of the 20th century was in the year 1972: 3.2 million barrels/day.

Table 102. Kuwait. Crude Oil Production and Reserves. 1970s.

Years	Production	% Change	Reserves	% Change
	thousands of barrels/ day		*millions of barrels*	
1970	2,989		68,000	
1971	3,196	6.9	67,100	-1.3
1972	3,283	2.7	66,023	-1.6
1973	3,020	-8.0	64,900	-1.7
1974	2,546	-15.7	64,000	-1.4
1975	2,084	-18.1	72,800	13.8
1976	2,145	2.9	68,000	-6.6
1977	1,969	-8.2	67,400	-0.9
1978	2,131	8.2	67,000	-0.6
1979	2,500	17.3	66,200	-1.2
1980	1,663	-33.5	65,400	-1.2
	Average Growth of Production		Average Growth of Reserves	
	-4.5		-0.3	

Sources: OPEC Annual Statistical Bulletin 1982; 1990.
Oil and Gas Journal 1999. Energy Statistics Sourcebook.

KUWAIT IN THE 1980S

Following the world trend of this decade, Kuwait's oil reserves grew faster than production, which fell.

Table 103. Kuwait. Crude Oil Production, Reserves and Consumption of Refined Products. 1980s.

Years	Production	% Change	Reserves	% Change	Consumption	% Change
	thousands of barrels/ day		*millions of barrels*		*thousands of barrels/day*	
1980	1,663		65,400			
1981	1,129	-32.1	67,730	3.6	56	—
1982	824	-27.0	67,150	-0.9	74	32.1
1983	1,054	27.9	67,000	-0.2	82	10.8
1984	1,053	-0.1	92,710	38.4	98	19.5
1985	936	-11.1	92,464	-0.3	95	-3.1
1986	1,237	32.2	94,522	2.2	96	1.1
1987	971	-21.5	94,525	0.0	85	-11.5
1988	1,396	43.8	94,525	0.0	75	-11.8
1989	1,463	4.8	97,125	2.8	72	-4.0
1990	1,177	-19.5	97,025	-0.1	65	-9.7
	Average Growth of Production		Average Growth of Reserves		Average Growth of Consumption	
	-0.3		4.5		2.6	

Source: OPEC Annual Statistical Bulletin 1982; 1984; 1985; 1990; 1999.

KUWAIT IN THE 1990S

In the 1990s the reserves showed a negative balance. On the other hand, the average production growth was 46.5%. In January of 1991, the Persian Gulf War erupted. Months before, Kuwait had been invaded by Iraq, which unleashed a counteroffensive by the Western countries. Petroleum production and reserves figures were no doubt influenced by the war; however, in the postwar years the reserves remained static while production returned to its previous growth rate. What does that mean? Why wouldn't the reserves grow to compensate for the production increase? Could it be because, in fact, the geologic possibilities of the region have begun to shrink? Kuwait is one of the world's most important producers, and for that reason Kuwait's statistics are especially significant. When reserves growth stagnates in the countries with the biggest reserves, like Kuwait, we must pay attention. Note also that to date Kuwait has not repeated its production peak reached in 1973.

Table 104. **Kuwait. Crude Oil Production, Reserves and Consumption of Refined Products.** 1990s.

Years	Production	% Change	Reserves	% Change	Consumption	% Change
	thousands of barrels/day		*Millions of barrels*		*thousands of barrels/day*	
1990	1,177		97,025		65	
1991	190	-83.8	96,955	-0.1	66	1.5
1992	1,057	456.0	96,568	-0.4	101	53.0
1993	1,881	78.0	96,500	-0.1	95	-5.9
1994	2,006	6.6	96,500	0.0	106	11.6
1995	2,006	0.0	96,500	0.0	117	10.4
1996	2,005	0.0	96,500	0.0	114	-2.6
1997	2,007	0.1	96,500	0.0	131	14.9
1998	2,051	2.2	96,500	0.0	158	20.6
1999	1,872	-8.7	96,500	0.0	163	3.2
2000	2,150	14.9	96,500	0.0	167	2.5
	Average Growth of Production		Average Growth of Reserves		Average Growth of Consumption	
	46.5		-0.1		10.9	

Source: OPEC Annual Statistical Bulletin 1990; 1995; 1999; 2000.

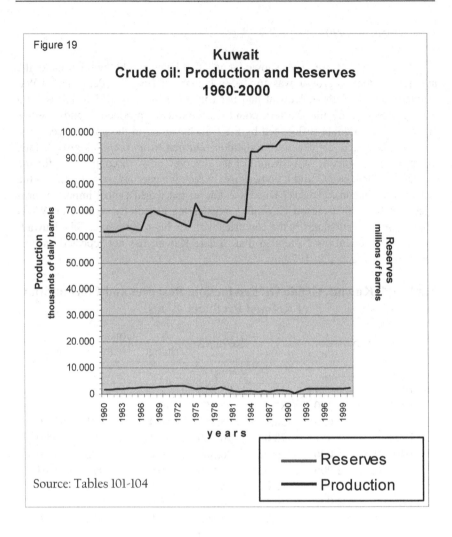

Figure 19

**Kuwait
Crude oil: Production and Reserves
1960-2000**

Source: Tables 101-104

Libya's average production growth was several times greater than the average reserves growth in the 1960s.

Table 105. Libya. Crude Oil Production and Reserves. 1960s.

Years	Production	% Change	Reserves	% Change
	thousands of barrels/ day		*Millions of barrels*	
1960	—		—	
1961	18		2,000	
1962	182	911.1	3,000	50.0
1963	441	142.3	4,500	50.0
1964	862	95.5	7,000	55.6
1965	1,218	41.3	9,000	28.6
1966	1,501	23.2	10,000	11.1
1967	1,740	15.9	20,000	100.0
1968	2,602	49.5	29,200	46.0
1969	3,109	19.5	30,000	2.7
1970	3,318	6.7	35,000	16.7
	Average Growth of Production		Average Growth of Reserves	
	145.0		40.1	

Sources: OPEC Annual Statistical Bulletin 1990.
Oil and Gas Journal 1999. Energy Statistics Sourcebook.

LIBYA IN THE 1970S

In the 1970s a sizable decrease of Libya's oil reserves was observed. At the same time, in 1970, Libya reached its maximum production level of the last forty years, 3.3 million barrels/day. In the first years of the decade Libyan leader Muhammad Kadhafi put pressure on the oil companies operating in that country to raise oil prices, which they did, a fact that would be the prelude to the 1973 Arab oil embargo.

Table 106. Libya. Crude Oil Production and Reserves. 1970s.

Years	Production	% Change	Reserves	% Change
	thousands of barrels/ day		*millions of barrels*	
1970	3,318		35,000	
1971	2,760	-16.8	29,200	-16.6
1972	2,239	-18.9	25,000	-14.4
1973	2,174	-2.9	30,400	21.6
1974	1,521	-30.0	25,500	-16.1
1975	1,479	-2.8	26,600	4.3
1976	1,932	30.6	26,100	-1.9
1977	2,063	6.8	25,500	-2.3
1978	1,982	-3.9	25,000	-2.0
1979	2,091	5.5	24,300	-2.8
1980	1,831	-12.4	23,500	-3.3
	Average Growth of Production		Average Growth of Reserves	
	-4.5		-3.3	

Sources: *OPEC Annual Statistical Bulletin 1990.*
Oil and Gas Journal 1999. Energy Statistics Sourcebook.

LIBYA IN THE 1980S

Unlike the other countries' reserves in this decade, Libya's remained about the same size. Production went a little down.

Table 107. Libya. Crude Oil Production and Reserves. 1980s.

Years	Production	% Change	Reserves	% Change	Consump-tion	% Change
	thousands of barrels/ day		*millions of barrels*		*thousands of barrels/day*	
1980	1,831		23,500		85	
1981	1,217	-33.5	22,600	-3.8	109	28.2
1982	1,136	-6.7	21,500	-4.9	98	-10.1
1983	1,104	-2.8	21,270	-1.1	104	6.1
1984	1,077	-2.4	21,100	-0.8	114	9.6
1985	1,023	-5.0	21,300	0.9	123	7.9
1986	1,308	27.9	22,800	7.0	94	-23.6
1987	972	-25.7	22,800	0.0	99	5.3
1988	1,029	5.9	22,800	0.0	104	5.1
1989	1,129	9.7	22,800	0.0	107	2.9
1990	1,388	22.9	22,935	0.6	100	-6.5
	Average Growth of Production		Average Growth of Reserves		Average Growth of Consumption	
	-1.0		-0.2		2.5	

Source: OPEC Annual Statistical Bulletin 1982; 1985, 1990, 1999

LIBYA IN THE 1990S

However, Libya's reserves went up significantly in the 1990s, while production stagnated. Consumption rose noticeably. This country reached its maximum production level of 3.3 million barrels/day and reserves at 35 million barrels in 1979. For the year 2000 the reserves show a recovery but it would be better to wait and see the trend.

Table 108. Libya. Crude Oil Production, Reserves and Consumption of Refined Products. 1990s.

Years	Production	% Change	Reserves	% Change	Consumption	% Change
	thousands of barrels/ day		*millions of barrels*		*thousands of barrels/day*	
1990	1,388		22,935		100	
1991	1,400	0.9	22,800	-0.6	105	5.0
1992	1,432	2.3	22,800	0.0	107	1.9
1993	1,361	-5.0	22,800	0.0	125	16.8
1994	1,389	2.1	22,800	0.0	153	22.4
1995	1,399	0.7	29,500	29.4	174	13.7
1996	1,394	-0.4	29,500	0.0	175	0.6
1997	1,395	0.1	29,500	0.0	174	-0.6
1998	1,449	3.9	29,500	0.0	170	-2.3
1999	1,287	-11.2	29,500	0.0	167	-1.8
2000	1,347	4.7	36,000	22.0	155	-7.2
	Average Growth of Production		Average Growth of Reserves		Average Growth of Consumption	
	-0.2		5.1		4.9	

Source: OPEC Annual Statistical Bulletin 1990; 1995; 1999; 2000.

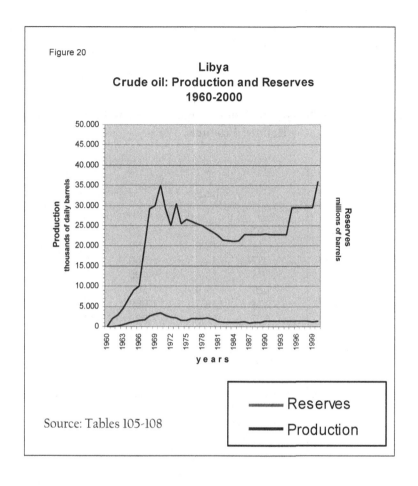

Figure 20

Libya
Crude oil: Production and Reserves
1960-2000

Source: Tables 105-108

NIGERIA IN THE 1960S

The Nigerian growth rate in the 1960s years was greater for production than for reserves.

Table 109. Nigeria. Crude Oil Production, Reserves and Consumption of Refined Products. 1960s.

Years	Production	% Change	Reserves	% Change
	thousands of barrels/ day		*millions of barrels*	
1960	17		80	
1961	46	170.6	150	
1962	67	45.7	300	100.0
1963	76	13.4	400	33.3
1964	120	57.9	500	25.0
1965	274	128.3	1,000	100.0
1966	417	52.2	3,000	200.0
1967	319	-23.5	3,500	16.7
1968	141	-55.8	3,550	1.4
1969	540	283.0	4,000	12.7
1970	1,083	100.6	5,000	25.0
	Average Growth of Production		Average Growth of Reserves	
	77.2		57.1	

Sources: OPEC Annual Statistical Bulletin 1990.
Oil and Gas Journal 1999. Energy Statistics Sourcebook.

NIGERIA IN THE 1970S

In the 1970s, Nigeria saw a strengthening of its reserves, which surpassed the average growth of production. In 1979, Nigeria reached its maximum oil production at 2.3 million barrels/day.

Table 110. Nigeria. Crude Oil Production, Reserves and Consumption of Refined Product**s. 1970s.**

Year	Production	% Change	Reserves	% Change	Consumption	% Change
	thousands of barrels/ day		Millions of barrels		thousands of barrels/day	
1970	1,083		5,000		28	
1971	1,531	41.4	9,300	86.0	34	21.4
1972	1,817	18.7	11,680	25.6	39	14.7
1973	2,054	13.0	15,000	28.4	48	23.1
1974	2,255	9.8	20,000	33.3	54	12.5
1975	1,783	-20.9	20,900	4.5	68	25.9
1976	2,066	15.9	20,200	-3.3	89	30.9
1977	2,085	0.9	19,500	-3.5	111	24.7
1978	1,897	-9.0	18,700	-4.1	134	20.7
1979	2,302	21.3	18,200	-2.7	154	14.9
1980	2,058	-10.6	17,400	-4.4	171	11.0
	Average Growth of Production		Average Growth of Reserves		Average Growth of Consumption	
	8.0		16.0		20.0	

Sources: OPEC Annual Statistical Bulletin 1981; 1990.
Oil and Gas Journal 1999. Energy Statistics Sourcebook.

In the 1980s the reserves began to diminish and production did likewise, supporting the theory that oil is running out.

Table 111. Nigeria. Crude Oil Production, Reserves and Consumption of Refined Products. **1980s.**

Years	Production	% Change	Reserves	% Change	Consumption	% Change
	thousands of barrels/day		*Millions of barrels*		*thousands of barrels/day*	
1980	2,058		17,400			
1981	1,439	-30.1	16,500	-5.2	235	
1982	1,287	-10.6	16,750	1.5	236	0.4
1983	1,235	-4.0	16,550	-1.2	225	-4.7
1984	1,388	12.4	16,650	0.6	203	-9.8
1985	1,498	7.9	16,600	-0.3	214	5.4
1986	1,466	-2.1	16,000	-3.6	196	-8.4
1987	1,323	-9.8	16,000	0.0	203	3.6
1988	1,340	1.3	16,000	0.0	220	8.4
1989	1,716	28.1	16,000	0.0	257	16.8
1990	1,726	0.6	17,100	6.9	291	13.2
	Average Growth of Production		Average Growth of Reserves		Average Growth of Consumption	
	-0.6		-0.1		2.8	

Source: OPEC Annual Statistical Bulletin 1982; 1990; 1999.

NIGERIA IN THE 1990S

Contrary to what was happening in the rest of the countries, in the 1990s Nigeria's reserves grew faster than production. This resulted in a net increase in the oil reserves of this country from 17 billion in 1990 to 22 billion in the year 2000.

Table 112. Nigeria. Crude Oil: Production, Reserves and Consumption of Refined Products. 1990s.

Year	Production	% Change	Reserves	% Change	Consumption	% Change
	thousands of barrels/day		*Millions of barrels*		*thousands of barrels/day*	
1990	1,726		17,100		291	
1991	1,893	9.7	20,000	17.0	234	-19.6
1992	1,957	3.4	20,990	5.0	244	4.3
1993	1,905	-2.7	20,990	0.0	211	-13.5
1994	1,821	-4.4	20,990	0.0	160	-24.2
1995	1,842	1.2	20,828	-0.8	186	16.3
1996	1,863	1.1	20,828	0.0	199	7.0
1997	1,876	0.7	20,828	0.0	200	0.5
1998	1,939	3.4	22,500	8.0	198	-1.0
1999	1,781	-8.1	22,500	0.0	184	-7.1
2000	2,053	15.3	22,500	0.0	—	—
	Average Growth of Production		Average Growth of Reserves		Average Growth of Consumption	
	1.9		2.9		-4.1	

Source: OPEC Annual Statistical Bulletin 1985; 1990; 2000.

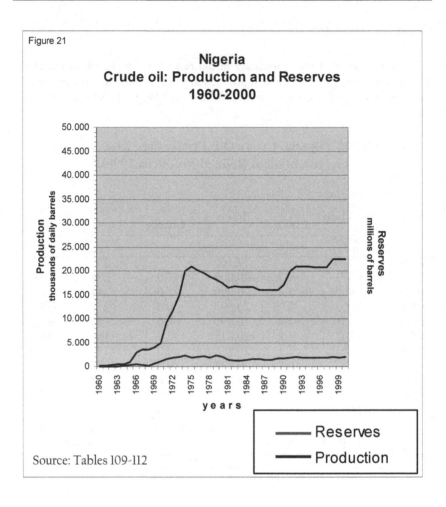

Figure 21

**Nigeria
Crude oil: Production and Reserves
1960-2000**

Source: Tables 109-112

QATAR IN THE 1960S

The reserves grew at a slightly better rate than production in this decade.

Table 113. Qatar. Crude Oil Production and Reserves. 1960s.

Year	Production	% Change	Reserves	% Change
	thousands of barrels/day		*Millions of barrels*	
1960	175		2,500	
1961	177	1.1	2,500	0.0
1962	186	5.1	2,750	10.0
1963	191	2.7	3,000	9.1
1964	215	12.6	2,950	-1.7
1965	232	7.9	3,500	18.6
1966	291	25.4	3,000	-14.3
1967	323	11.0	4,000	33.3
1968	339	5.0	3,750	-6.3
1969	355	4.7	3,875	3.3
1970	362	2.0	5,500	41.9
Average Growth		7.7		9.4

Sources: *OPEC Annual Statistical Bulletin 1990*
Oil and Gas Journal 1999. Energy Statistics Sourcebook.

QATAR IN THE 1970S

In these years the reserves diminished sharply while production grew significantly. In other words, the reserves were being drawn down.

Table 114. Qatar. Crude Oil Production, Reserves and Consumption of Refined Products. 1970s.

Years	Production	% Change	Reserves	% Change	Consumption	% Change
	thousands of barrels/day		*millions of barrels*		*thousands of barrels/day*	
1970	362		5,500		1	
1971	431	19.1	4,300	-21.8	1	0.0
1972	482	11.8	6,000	39.5	2	100.0
1973	570	18.3	7,000	16.7	2	0.0
1974	518	-9.1	6,500	-7.1	3	50.0
1975	438	-15.4	6,000	-7.7	4	33.3
1976	497	13.5	5,850	-2.5	5	25.0
1977	445	-10.5	5,700	-2.6	7	40.0
1978	487	9.4	5,600	-1.8	7	0.0
1979	508	4.3	4,000	-28.6	8	14.3
1980	471	-7.3	3,700	-7.5	9	12.5
	Average Growth of Production		Average Growth of Reserves		Average Growth of Consumption	
	3.4		-2.3		27.5	

Sources: OPEC Annual Statistical Bulletin 1981; 1982; 1990.
Oil and Gas Journal 1999. Energy Statistics Sourcebook.

QATAR IN THE 1980S

Qatar followed the global trend and recorded greater growth of reserves than of production in the 1980s. The reserves figures were much stronger in this decade.

Table 115. Qatar. Crude Oil Production, Reserves and Consumption of Refined Products. 1980s.

Years	Produc-tion	% Change	Reserves	% Change	Consump-tion	% Change
	thousands of barrels/day		*millions of barrels*		*thousands of barrels/day*	
1980	471		3,700			
1981	415	-11.9	3,434	-7.2	10	
1982	332	-20.0	3,425	-0.3	11	10.0
1983	269	-19.0	3,330	-2.8	12	9.1
1984	325	20.8	4,500	35.1	12	0.0
1985	290	-10.8	4,500	0.0	12	0.0
1986	314	8.3	4,500	0.0	11	-8.3
1987	291	-7.3	4,500	0.0	11	0.0
1988	319	9.6	4,500	0.0	12	9.1
1989	320	0.3	4,500	0.0	13	8.3
1990	406	26.9	4,500	0.0	13	0.0
	Average Growth of Production		Average Growth of Reserves		Average Growth of Consumption	
	-0.3		2.5		3.1	

Source: OPEC Annual Statistical Bulletin 1985; 1990.

QATAR IN THE 1990S

In 2000, Qatar reached the peak of its production to that date. The reserves were also increased during this decade to a new high of 13 billion barrels, after going through a period of stagnation.

Table 116. Qatar. Crude Oil Production, Reserves and Consumption of Refined Products. 1990s.

Years	Production	% Change	Reserves	% Change	Consumption	% Change
	thousands of barrels/day		*Millions of barrels*		*thousands of barrels/day*	
1990	406		4,500		13	
1991	391	-3.7	2,993	-33.5	12	-7.7
1992	423	8.2	3,121	4.3	13	8.3
1993	390	-7.8	3,121	0.0	14	7.7
1994	378	-3.1	3,500	12.1	16	14.3
1995	390	3.2	3,700	5.7	17	6.3
1996	393	0.8	3,700	0.0	19	11.8
1997	405	3.1	3,700	0.0	21	10.5
1998	618	52.6	3,700	0.0	23	9.5
1999	608	-1.6	3,700	0.0	22	-4.3
2000	648	6.6	13,100	254.1	23	4.5
	Average Growth of Production		Average Growth of Reserves		Average Growth of Consumption	
	5.8		24.3		6.1	

Source: OPEC Annual Statistical Bulletin 1990; 1999; 2000.

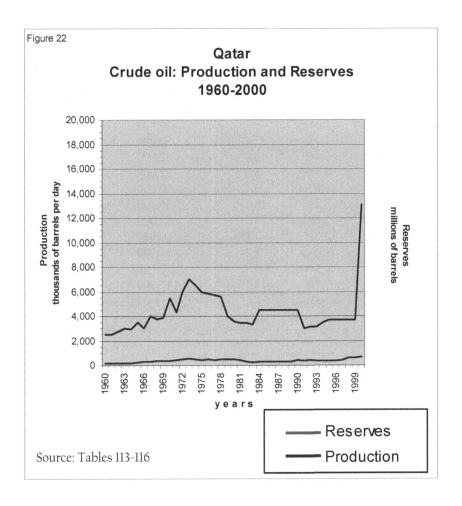

Figure 22

Qatar
Crude oil: Production and Reserves
1960-2000

Source: Tables 113-116

In the Sixties there was a net increase of the Saudi reserves.

Table 117. Saudi Arabia. Crude Oil Production and Reserves. 1960s.

Years	Production	% Change	Reserves	% Change
	thousands of barrels/day		*millions of barrels*	
1960	1,313		50,000	
1961	1,480	12.7	50,000	0.0
1962	1,642	10.9	52,000	4.0
1963	1,786	8.8	52,000	0.0
1964	1,896	6.2	60,000	15.4
1965	2,205	16.3	60,500	0.8
1966	2,601	18.0	60,000	-0.8
1967	2,805	7.8	66,000	10.0
1968	3,042	8.4	74,700	13.2
1969	3,216	5.7	77,000	3.1
1970	3,799	18.1	140,000	81.8
	Average Growth of Production		Average Growth of Reserves	
	11.3		12.7	

Sources: OPEC Annual Statistical Bulletin 1990.
Oil and Gas Journal 1999. Energy Statistics Sourcebook.

SAUDI ARABIA IN THE 1970S

Then, reserves grew at a slower rate than production, so that the trend observed in the previous decade was reversed.

Table 118. Saudi Arabia. Crude Oil Production and Reserves. 1970s.

Years	Production	% Change	Reserves	% Change
	thousands of barrels/day		*Millions of barrels*	
1970	3,799		140,000	
1971	4,768	25.5	128,500	-8.2
1972	6,016	26.2	145,300	13.1
1973	7,596	26.3	138,000	-5.0
1974	8,479	11.6	132,000	-4.3
1975	7,075	-16.6	164,500	24.6
1976	8,577	21.2	148,600	-9.7
1977	9,199	7.3	151,400	1.9
1978	8,301	-9.8	150,000	-0.9
1979	9,532	14.8	165,700	10.5
1980	9,900	3.9	163,350	-1.4
	Average Growth of Production		Average Growth of Reserves	
	11.0		2.0	

Sources: OPEC Annual Statistical Bulletin 1990. Oil and Gas Journal 1999. Energy Statistics Sourcebook.

In 1980, Saudi Arabia hit its production peak for the century at 9.9 million barrels/day. From then until 2000, production went down and up again, but it never surpassed the high point of 1980. In line with the trend elsewhere, Saudi Arabia also increased its reserves significantly.

Table 119. Saudi Arabia. Crude Oil Production, Reserves and Consumption of Refined Products. 1980s.

Years	Production	% Change	Reserves	% Change	Consump- tion	% Change
	thousands of barrels/day		*Millions of barrels*		*thousands of barrels/day*	
1980	9,900		163,300			
1981	9,808	-0.9	167,850	2.8	416	
1982	6,483	-33.9	165,320	-1.5	451	8.4
1983	4,539	-30.0	168,848	2.1	478	6.0
1984	4,079	-10.1	171,710	1.7	489	2.3
1985	3,175	-22.2	171,490	-0.1	516	5.5
1986	4,784	50.7	169,179	-1.3	621	20.3
1987	3,975	-16.9	169,585	0.2	632	1.8
1988	5,090	28.1	254,989	50.4	685	8.4
1989	5,064	-0.5	260,050	2.0	701	2.3
1990	6,412	26.6	260,004	0.0	733	4.6
	Average Growth of Production		Average Growth of Reserves		Average Growth of Consumption	
	-0.9		5.6		6.6	

Source: OPEC Annual Statistical Bulletin 1982; 1985; 1990; 1999.

SAUDI ARABIA IN THE 1990S

In the 1990s, the situation changed completely. The reserves practically stood still, registering an increment of less than one percent, on average, during the decade. Production, in contrast, grew 2.7%. In other words, Saudi Arabia was extracting more oil than was being discovered. This situation takes on a special connotation, given that this country is the world's largest producer and has the world's greatest oil reserves. If the supply is diminishing here, it is plain that the world really is running out of oil.

Table 120. Saudi Arabia. Crude Oil Production, Reserves and Consumption of Refined Products. 1990s.

Years	Production	% Change	Reserves	% Change	Consumption	% Change
	thousands of barrels/day		*millions of barrels*		*thousands of barrels/day*	
1990	6,412		260,004		733	
1991	8,117	26.6	260,936	0.4	676	-7.8
1992	8,331	2.6	261,203	0.1	729	7.8
1993	8,047	-3.4	261,203	0.0	767	5.2
1994	8,049	0.0	261,374	0.1	792	3.3
1995	8,023	-0.3	261,450	0.0	751	-5.2
1996	8,102	1.0	261,444	0.0	807	7.5
1997	8,011	-1.1	261,541	0.0	814	0.9
1998	8,280	3.4	261,542	0.0	865	6.3
1999	7,564	-8.6	262,784	0.5	908	5.0
2000	8,094	7.0	262,700	0.0	937	3.2
	Average Growth of Production		Average Growth of Reserves		Average Growth of Consumption	
	2.7		0.1		2.6	

Source: OPEC Annual Statistical Bulletin 1995; 1999; 2000.

171

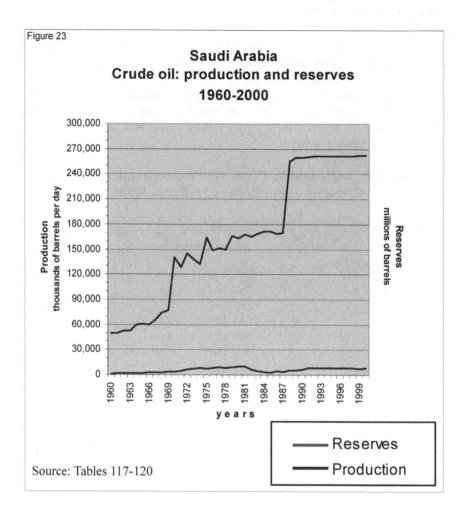

Figure 23

Saudi Arabia
Crude oil: production and reserves
1960-2000

Source: Tables 117-120

UNITED ARAB EMIRATES IN THE 1960S

The 1960s was a period of great growth for the UAE, in terms of production and for reserves as well.

Table 121. United Arab Emirates. Crude Oil Production and Reserves. 1960s.

Years	Production	% Change	Reserves	% Change
	thousands of barrels/day		*millions of barrels*	
1961			250	
1962	14		3,500	1,300.0
1963	48	242.9	5,000	42.9
1964	186	287.5	7,500	50.0
1965	282	51.6	7,700	2.7
1966	360	27.7	10,000	29.9
1967	382	6.1	12,500	25.0
1968	496	29.8	15,000	20.0
1969	627	26.4	18,000	20.0
1970	779	24.2	16,000	-11.1
	Average Growth of Production		Average Growth of Reserves	
	87.0		164.4	

Sources: *OPEC Annual Statistical Bulletin 1990.*
Oil and Gas Journal 1999. Energy Statistics Sourcebook.

UNITED ARAB EMIRATES IN THE 1970S

Both production and reserves growth showed a clear drop in the 1970s, from an average growth rate of 87% to only 9% for production and from 164.4% on average to 8.1% for reserves.

Table 122. United Arab Emirates. Crude Oil Production and Reserves. 1970s.

Years	Production	% Change	Reserves	% Change
	thousands of barrels/day		*millions of barrels*	
1970	779		16,000	
1971	1,059	35.9	11,800	-26.3
1972	1,202	13.5	18,948	60.6
1973	1,532	27.5	20,768	9.6
1974	1,678	9.5	21,500	3.5
1975	1,663	-0.9	30,000	39.5
1976	1,930	16.1	29,500	-1.7
1977	1,998	3.5	29,000	-1.7
1978	1,830	-8.4	31,000	6.9
1979	1,830	0.0	30,000	-3.2
1980	1,701	-7.0	28,000	-6.7
	Average Growth of Production		Average Growth of Reserves	
	9.0		8.1	

Sources: *OPEC Annual Statistical Bulletin 1990.*
Oil and Gas Journal 1999. Energy Statistics Sourcebook.

UNITED ARAB EMIRATES IN THE 1980S

The 1980s looked good almost everywhere. In the UAE, production went down, while reserves tripled.

Table 123. United Arab Emirates. Crude Oil Production, Reserves and Consumption of Refined Products. 1980s.

Years	Production	% Change	Reserves	% Change	Consumption	% Change
	thousands of barrels/day		*Millions of barrels*		*thousands of barrels/day*	
1980	1,701		28,000			
1981	1,502	-11.70	32,176	14.91	78	
1982	1,248	-16.91	32,354	0.55	71	-8.97
1983	1,149	-7.93	32,340	-0.04	78	9.86
1984	1,069	-6.96	32,490	0.46	79	1.28
1985	1,012	-5.33	32,990	1.54	83	5.06
1986	1,146	13.24	97,203	194.64	102	22.89
1987	1,281	11.78	98,105	0.93	109	6.86
1988	1,359	6.09	98,105	0.00	112	2.75
1989	1,641	20.75	98,105	0.00	114	1.79
1990	1,818	10.79	98,100	-0.01	115	0.88
	Average Growth of Production		Average Growth of Reserves		Average Growth of Consumption	
	1.4		21.3		4.7	

Source: OPEC Annual Statistical Bulletin 1985; 1990.

175

UNITED ARAB EMIRATES IN THE 1990S

Then came clear evidence that the reserves were stagnating. The trend of the previous years was abruptly broken. In the 1960s, the UAE reserves had grown on average by 164.4%; in the 1970s by 8.1%; in the 1980s by 21.3%; and in the 1990s they stopped growing altogether. This was consistent with results the world over during the 1990s; oil reserves did not maintain their growth rates during the last years of the 20th century.

Another of the largest producer countries began to show signs that its oil supplies were being exhausted.

Table 124. United Arab Emirates. Crude Oil: Production, Reserves and Consumption of Refined Products. 1990s.

Years	Production	% Change	Reserves	% Change	Consumption	% Change
	thousands of barrels/day		*millions of barrels*		*thousands of barrels/day*	
1990	1,818		98,100		115	
1991	2,093	15.13	98,100	0.00	118	2.61
1992	2,241	7.07	98,100	0.00	124	5.08
1993	2,159	-3.66	98,100	0.00	133	7.26
1994	2,166	0.32	98,100	0.00	132	-0.75
1995	2,148	-0.83	98,100	0.00	125	-5.30
1996	2,161	0.61	97,800	-0.31	123	-1.60
1997	2,160	-0.05	97,800	0.00	115	-6.50
1998	2,244	3.89	97,800	0.00	130	13.04
1999	2,048	-8.73	97,800	0.00	127	-2.31
2000	2,174	—	97,800	—	135	—
	Average Growth of Production		Average Growth of Reserves		Average Growth of Consumption	
	1.5		0.0		1.3	

Source: OPEC Annual Statistical Bulletin 1990; 1995; 1999; 2000.

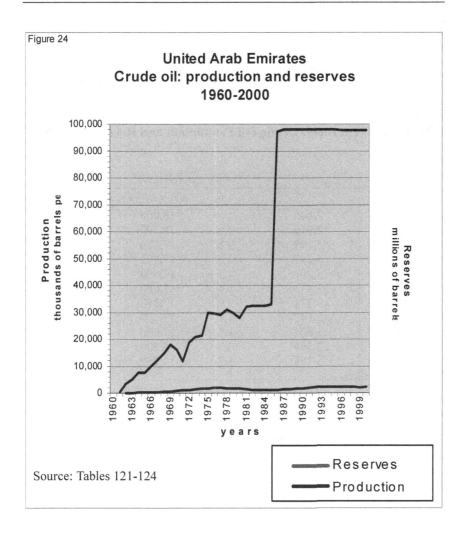

Figure 24

United Arab Emirates
Crude oil: production and reserves
1960-2000

Source: Tables 121-124

VENEZUELA IN THE 1960S

In Venezuela, production grew faster than reserves in the 1960s, so that reserves diminished significantly, from 18 billion barrels in 1960 to 14.8 billion barrels in 1970s.

Table 125. Venezuela. Crude Oil Production and Reserves. 1960s.

Years	Production	% Change	Reserves	% Change
	thousands of barrels/day		*millions of barrels*	
1960	2,846		18,000	
1961	2,919	2.6	18,500	2.8
1962	3,199	9.6	17,550	-5.1
1963	3,247	1.5	17,000	-3.1
1964	3,392	4.5	17,000	0.0
1965	3,472	2.4	17,000	0.0
1966	3,371	-2.9	17,250	1.5
1967	3,542	5.1	17,400	0.9
1968	3,604	1.8	17,000	-2.3
1969	3,594	-0.3	15,500	-8.8
1970	3,708	3.2	14,750	-4.8
	Average Growth of Production		Average Growth of Reserves	
	2.7		-1.9	

Sources: OPEC Annual Statistical Bulletin 1990. Page 53.
Oil and Gas Journal 1999. Energy Statistics Sourcebook. P. 153

VENEZUELA IN THE 1970S

In the next decade production diminished by 4.9%, on average, while the reserves were increased by 3%. In 1970, Venezuela reached its highest level of oil production in the 20th century, 3.7 million barrels/day. In 1973, the Arab oil embargo that was put in place as a consequence of the Yom Kippur War elevated oil prices to levels never seen before.

Table 126. Venezuela. Crude Oil: Production and Reserves. 1970s.

Years	Production	% Change	Reserves	% Change
	thousands of barrels/day		*millions of barrels*	
1970	3,708		14,750	
1971	3,549	-4.3	14,000	-5.1
1972	3,219	-9.3	13,900	-0.7
1973	3,366	4.6	13,700	-1.4
1974	2,976	-11.6	14,000	2.2
1975	2,346	-21.2	15,000	7.1
1976	2,294	-2.2	17,700	18.0
1977	2,237	-2.5	18,039	1.9
1978	2,165	-3.2	18,228	1.0
1979	2,356	8.8	18,523	1.6
1980	2,165	-8.1	19,530	5.4
	Average Growth of Production		Average Growth of Reserves	
	-4.9		3.0	

Sources: OPEC Annual Statistical Bulletin 1982; 1990.
Oil and Gas Journal 1999. Energy Statistics Sourcebook.

VENEZUELA IN THE 1980S

In this period, following the world trend, the Venezuelan oil reserves jumped from 19.5 million barrels in 1980 to 60.1 million barrels in 1990; they tripled in a ten-year period. The greatest increment took place between 1985 and 1986, when the reserves were doubled due to the incorporation of part of the nonconventional oil of the Orinoco Belt into the reserves figures.

Table 127. Venezuela. Crude oil: Production, Reserves and Consumption of Refined Products. 1980s.

Years	Production	% Change	Reserves	% Change	Consump-tion	% Change
	thousands of barrels/day		*Millions of barrels*		*thousands of barrels/day*	
1980	2,165		19,530			
1981	2,108	-2.6	19,888	1.8	389	
1982	1,895	-10.1	24,900	25.2	391	0.5
1983	1,800	-5.0	25,887	4.0	384	-1.8
1984	1,695	-5.8	28,028	8.3	352	-8.3
1985	1,564	-7.7	27,200	-3.0	355	0.9
1986	1,648	5.4	55,521	104.1	375	5.6
1987	1,575	-4.4	58,101	4.6	377	0.5
1988	1,578	0.2	58,505	0.7	386	2.4
1989	1,747	10.7	59,040	0.9	367	-4.9
1990	2,135	22.2	60,054	1.7	374	1.9
	Average Growth of Production		Average Growth of Reserves		Average Growth of Consumption	
	0.3		14.8		-0.4	

Source: OPEC Annual Statistical Bulletin 1982; 1985; 1990; 1999.

VENEZUELA IN THE 1990S

In the 1990s, the situation changed completely. Production grew on average 3.5%, while the reserves grew only by 2.5%.

Table 128. Venezuela. Crude Oil Production, Reserves and Consumption of Refined Products. 1990s.

Years	Production	% Change	Reserves	% Change	Consump-tion	% Change
	thousands of barrels/day		*Millions of barrels*		*thousands of barrels/day*	
1990	2,135		60,054		374	
1991	2,286	7.1	62,649	4.3	379	1.3
1992	2,345	2.6	63,330	1.1	402	6.1
1993	2,326	-0.8	64,448	1.8	419	4.2
1994	2,367	1.8	64,877	0.7	412	-1.7
1995	2,378	0.5	66,329	2.2	416	1.0
1996	2,381	0.1	72,667	9.6	403	-3.1
1997	2,411	1.3	74,930	3.1	411	2.0
1998	3,120	29.4	76,108	1.6	441	7.3
1999	2,800	-10.3	76,848	1.0	383	-13.2
2000	2,891	3.3	76,800	-0.1	410	7.0
	Average Growth of Production		Average Growth of Reserves		Average Growth of Consumption	
	3.5		2.5		1.1	

Source: OPEC Annual Statistical Bulletin 1989; 1990; 1995; 1999; 2000.

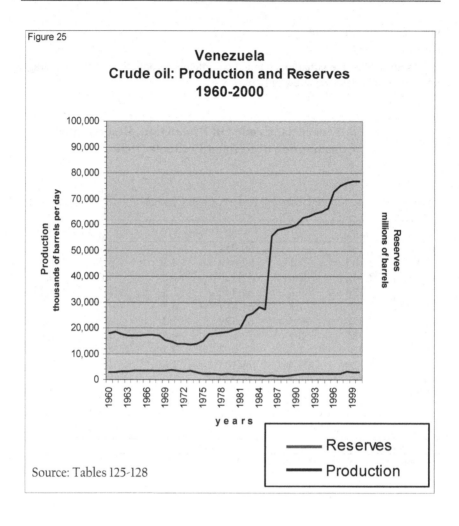

Figure 25

**Venezuela
Crude oil: Production and Reserves
1960-2000**

Source: Tables 125-128

CONCLUSION ON OPEC COUNTRIES

The decrease in oil reserves of most of the members of the OPEC is a reality. Algeria appears to have stagnated, since its reserves hovered in the 11.3 billion barrel range throughout the last several years of the 20th century and have not moved up significantly since then. Indonesia's reserves fell by more than 50% in the 1990s, from 11.1 billion barrels in 1990 to 5.1 million barrels in 2000. Estimates for 2004 put the reserves at 4.9 billion. Iran and Iraq's reserves stayed pretty much the same; Libya was also basically stagnated although between 1999 and the year 2000 it achieved a recovery. Nigeria had a moderate growth in the last two years of the century. Qatar was stagnated, although in 1999 its reserves leapt from 3.7 billion barrels to 13.1 million barrels in 2000, an increase of 255.6% in one year. Meanwhile, the Saudi Arabian reserves remained stagnated at around 262 billion barrels. In the United Arab Emirates, production went up slightly in the 1990s but the reserves remained stagnated. Kuwait's reserves stayed around 96.5 billion barrels. In Venezuela for the whole decade of the 1990s and especially in the last three years, the reserves failed to grow. Calculating current reserves is tricky in any event. As David R. Francis wrote in the *Christian Science Monitor*,[30] "The Royal Dutch/Shell Group, one of the world's largest oil producers, shocked the financial community ... when it announced it had overbooked its proven reserves by 20 percent — an indication of the fragility of such estimates."While some countries may have squeezed something more out of the ground in the first part of the 2000s, many of the OPEC countries reached their highest production levels of the 20th century *in the 1970s*. The statistics analyzed in this chapter show a clear trend of stagnation and decreasing oil reserves while production continues to go up, a phenomenon that is obviously unsustainable in the long run. The US Secretary of Energy estimates that oil world consumption will grow by more than 50% from 73 million barrels/day in 1997 to 112 million barrels/day in 2020.

How can anyone pretend that the geological reality will enable us to continue producing oil at even the current rate?

Nonconventional Oil

The shrinking of the reserves of conventional oil and the development of technology in recent years have made it more desirable and more feasible to make better use of the nonconventional oil reserves that exist. Nonconventional oil is found in two states in nature: as a liquid (and therefore capable of being extracted from wells), and in the form of rocks and sands impregnated with hydrocarbons. In the first case it is relatively easy to extract using a process

---

30. "Has global oil production peaked?" January 29, 2004 edition online at http://www.csmonitor.com/2004/0129/p14s01-wogi.html

similar to the one used for obtaining conventional oil. In the second case, it is much more difficult. The process basically amounts to mining oil, since it is necessary to process the sands or to cut the rocks impregnated with oil and to subject them to heat in order to obtain the hydrocarbons. There is a great qualitative difference between oil produced from conventional wells and that obtained from the mining of oil. Most of the nonconventional oil reserves known today are of the second type. They are to a large extent found in Canada, Siberia, China and in the United States.

THE ORINOCO BELT — THE LARGEST RESERVE

But there is one region that outweighs the rest. It is the Orinoco Belt, located in the east of Venezuela, where the reserves of heavy oil are estimated at 100-270 billion barrels. Of that quantity, Venezuela has already incorporated into its proven reserves 32.9 billion barrels of extra heavy crude and 2.7 billion barrels of bitumen.[31] If we add to Venezuela's 77.6 billions barrels of proven reserves for 2000 a conservative figure of 120 billion barrels of possible and probable reserves of the Orinoco Belt, this country would have 197 billion barrels of profitable oil reserves. The incorporation of Venezuela's nonconventional reserves would not significantly modify the world reserves figures but it does make Venezuela the second place holder of oil reserves.

In the 1990s, some sectors had been trying to buy part of the Venezuelan oil company, PDVSA, an operation that was one of the largest businesses in the world as of the beginning of the 21st century, at least in terms of the magnitude of future benefits that it would generate. The real value of PDVSA is more than $2 trillion. The value of an oil or mining company is not determined by its fixed assets nor its cash flow at a given moment, but its profitable reserves. The value of PDVSA was estimated at $150 billion in the 1990s, a figure that does not represent a fraction of its real value. Its proven oil reserves alone were recorded at $77.6 billion barrels in 2000. At the lowest price in the market, say $10 per barrel, the value of PDVSA would be more like $776 billion. But if we add the 120 billion barrels of probable and possible reserves in the Orinoco Belt to the PDVSA patrimony, then the scale changes entirely. Now we are talking about 197.6 billion barrels; at $10 dollars per barrel this is almost $2 trillion, at the very least. And, of course, if we use the August 2005 price of $60 per barrel, then we have a total value of $12 trillion.

Thus, the valuation of PDVSA at $150 billion seems to take into account only 7.5% of its minimum value. Based on that valuation the party interested in acquiring PDVSA offered to buy one-third of the company, for which it would

---

31. Venezuela Energy and Mines Ministry. Oil and Natural Gas Reserves to December 31, 2000, tables 4 and 12. General Direction of Hydrocarbons.

pay $50 billion. This is equivalent to paying $0.25 per barrel of oil (taking as a base the proven reserves of 77.6 billion barrels plus the 120 billion barrels of probable and possible reserves of the Orinoco Belt.) That would have been a very good deal. For someone. No wonder the possible sale of a piece of PDVSA attracted the interest of so many oil experts, lawyers and economists.

Extra Heavy Oil as a Source of Uranium, Gold and Other Minerals

There is another important feature to extra heavy oil. Tests have shown that uranium, gold, vanadium and other valuable materials have been found in the residuals of the Orinoco Belt heavy oil.

The Orinoco Oil Belt is located across the Orinoco River from the Guayana Region. Guayana is one of the richest mining areas in the world. This is the place where the Spanish conquistadors found the legendary "El Dorado," a region where gold practically lay exposed for the picking on the earth's surface. This whole immense area today it is exploited on a grand scale for gold and diamonds. But the wealth is not limited to these two minerals. And this is the same geologic basin that holds the Orinoco Belt, so that it is reasonable to suppose that at least some of the same natural resources that exist in Guayana will also be available in Orinoco.

CHAPTER 11. A DIFFERENT OPTION

Although an objective statistical analysis points to the conclusion that oil reserves cannot be increased sufficiently to restore the production rate reached during the last decade of the 20th century, and that oil can run out and sooner or later must run out, many experts and institutions refuse to accept this view. After all, there are still numerous geological regions in the world with probable reserves that have not been measured; there is in any case a considerable quantity of oil yet to be discovered.

Other experts suggest that the world will gradually become less dependent on oil as we develop alternative energy sources and more energy-efficient technologies, that is, when we learn to produce the same results using a smaller quantity of energy. The industrialized world has had some relative success in developing alternative fuels and more efficient processes, but it is the less-developed countries where the greatest growth in fuel consumption is expected. Even in the West, dependence on petroleum will be mitigated only slightly by the substitution of different sources like gas, solar energy, eolic energy, biomass, hydroelectricity, nuclear energy and hydrogen.

WILL HIGH OIL PRICES SLOW THE USE OF OIL?

Some experts suggest that as soon as the price of oil reaches a certain point, other energy sources will become more economical and will automatically take its place. According to this thesis, the only reason for oil's current dominance in the energy market is that it is still more economical than the other resources. But this theory is not completely correct. If it were, oil would have been displaced many years ago. The truth is that oil continues as the predominant energy source because no one has found an appropriate substitute.

The problem is not only the monetary cost but the practicality of the alternatives. The ways in which an energy source can be used vary with the weight, the
volume and the physical state of the resource. Solar energy for the most part has
not been collected in a form that is of sufficient intensity for many applications;
this means that a far greater investment is required to obtain a certain result than
if other alternatives were used. For that reason, the production of solar energy has
been much more expensive than oil and coal, and it is also difficult to store and
conserve. Nuclear energy and the applications of biomass also present significant
inconveniences. The enormity of the risk that attends any possible nuclear
accident and the conundrum of what to do with the waste from nuclear power
plants cannot be ignored. The use of biomass generates serious problems of contamination derived from the burning of those resources, which produce great
quantities of smoke, contributing to the greenhouse effect and the deterioration of
the ozone layer, among other things. The National Renewable Energy Laboratory
(NREL is a national laboratory of the U.S. Department of Energy) explains that
"biomass [or bioenergy] is plant matter such as trees, grasses, agricultural crops
or other biological material. It can be used as a solid fuel, or converted into liquid
or gaseous forms, for the production of electric power, heat, chemicals, or fuels."
However, despite ongoing research efforts, biomass does not generate high-
intensity energy and it entails the clearing of forests and the burning of great
quantities of organic material, with the attendant risks of altering the ecological
balance of the regions where it is practiced.

Hydroelectric energy and natural gas are two alternative energy sources that
currently appear to be less polluting, yet they offer appropriate energy intensity
for use in the generation of electricity and of heat. Natural gas is being used
experimentally in transportation applications including city buses and trucks, but
it has not had enough success to catch on. Oil continues to be the primary energy
source.

THE YAMANI VISION

Reuters reported on September 5, 2000, that the former Saudi Arabian oil
minister, Ahmed Zaki Yamani, said that OPEC would pay a high price for having
failed to act to avoid an elevation of oil prices in 1999. Affirming that the Stone
Age did not end because the world ran out of stones, he predicted that the Oil
Age would not end because we ran out of oil; rather, he said, technological innovations will reduce oil consumption and will increase the productive capacity of
the non-OPEC countries. In other words, before all the oil is gone, as prices go
higher, other energy sources will become more competitive.

Many important figures consider that oil will never be completely out of the
picture. They think that the question of using up the reserves is just a matter of
gradually using up the most convenient and accessible reserves, that is, the oil

that is easy to extract and therefore less costly than its substitutes. In other words, it is the price of oil that will determine whether and when it will be replaced. If the price rises so high that other fuels become more economical, then other fuels will be used.

However, this idea has been around for a long time and still the search goes on. None of the alternative sources of energy known to date can take the place of petroleum. It takes a lot of coal to produce the energy potential of one gallon of gasoline, for example, and coal is very bulky. And besides, petroleum products are safer and easier to use; they are less dangerous than other sources like natural gas and nuclear energy.

The electric automobile has not been successful because no one has been able to develop an energy potential giving it the same power as a gas motor. Nor have vehicles powered by sugar-cane alcohol been successful.

In the last few years, many breakthroughs have been announced with regard to the use of hydrogen to power cars and other vehicles. If such vehicles can be put into production, the impact on oil consumption would be tremendous. This in itself would be an important step. But up to now it is only an experimental project.

TECHNOLOGY TRANSFERS — EXPORTING THE BIGGEST POLLUTERS TO THE THIRD WORLD

In spite of all such innovative efforts to discover non-polluting technologies, the reality is that these efforts relate only to the big industrial countries and they do not reach the less-developed countries. For example, in the 1970s the North American automobile industry switched away from building engines that use gasoline with lead; now they only build for no-lead gas. The plants that produced the old-style motors were moved out of the United States and transferred to other regions like Latin America, where they continue building motors for leaded gasoline, thirty years on.

Third World countries were glad to accept any automobile plant at all, and cannot afford to turn up their noses just because of a bit of pollution. Ironically, many refineries of the undeveloped countries were already designed to produce unleaded gasoline but were forced to acquire sulfur to mix with the gasoline for the domestic market. This means that they had no alternative but to contaminate their own gasoline. Thus, there is no coherent effort in the world to diminish the contamination to acceptable levels — only to keep it in the Third World.

Conclusion on the Divergent Positions

The search for a substitute for oil has been going on at least from the late 1930s and the 1940s, when in the middle of the Second World War Germany worked to produce alternative fuels but had only limited success. After the Arab oil embargo in 1973 and 1979, the big consumer nations have also tried to find substitutes and have achieved some success in certain areas, like the production of electricity by the use of nuclear energy, but at a high environmental cost. The big consumers have also managed to reduce their consumption in relative terms. But in the rest of the world the demand for oil is still heating up. Oil is in no danger of going out of style anytime soon.

To accept the idea that this invaluable commodity might run out very soon is to accept a kind of apocalyptic vision of this century. It seems easier to pretend that oil is infinite; that it can be replaced; that great new reserves are sure to be found any day now. Just as they used to think that the gold in California would never run out.

There is no global organization that audits and certifies the existing reserves. The statistics that are officially disclosed depend on the good faith of the countries and the companies doing the reporting. Some specialists and institutions have expressed doubts about the reserves figures that are officially reported. For example, the estimated oil resources of the Caspian Sea may have been exaggerated. There are great disparities between the estimates made by private companies and those formulated by the United States Department of Energy. Washington may have an interest in highlighting the importance of alternatives to the Persian Gulf producers, in order to play down that region's apparent strategic importance.

Specialized institutions in the strategic and political field have also expressed wonder about many of the figures published by official institutions of certain countries. Reports that fundamentally lack credibility create reasonable doubts about the truthfulness of all information that is published regarding reserves. But they are only doubts. There is no irrefutable test that can be used to verify whether the reported reserves correspond at all with reality.

In any case, since oil is a strategic product of the first magnitude, as important or more important than any defense system or weapon, it is reasonable to assume that many of the statistics are intentionally fudged. Countries surely disclose information about their reserves according to their own political and/or strategic interests. Oil is closely linked with national security and power in every country. There is every reason to think that the official figures on oil reserves are imprecise at best. Whether they are overestimated or underestimated would depend on how each country perceives its own interest. Estimating high tends to magnify the apparent supply and to avoid price increases. Estimating low could encourage price hikes on the basis of a perceived potential shortage. Although most nations, both consumers and producers, had arrived at an implicit agreement to maintain prices within a certain corridor in order to help stabilize the operation of the world economy, since 1999 that agreement has been broken and oil prices have fluctuated considerably.

Regardless of the accuracy of any one set of reported statistics, the overall trend suggests that the total oil supply is being drained down in the entire world and that new reserves are not being discovered in sufficient quantity to restore the amounts of oil the world now produces and consumes.

CHAPTER 12. HOW LONG WILL THE OIL RESERVES LAST?

In 2000, the world's oil reserves reached 1,077,500 million barrels.[32] With production running at 65.8 million barrels/day (2000)[33], the reserves would last for 16,375 days. That is to say, for about 44 years, assuming no significant new reserves are found and assuming production stayed at same rate. But in reality, as seen in Chapter 2, consumption is projected to increase steeply. If the estimates of the United States Department of Energy are correct, world consumption in 2005 must be around 83.9 million barrels/day,[34] that is to say, approximately 10 million barrels more than in 1997. Supposing that production is equal to the projected consumption of 83.9 million barrels/day and supposing that the reserves maintain the same stable trend shown in the 1990s — and taking the figure of the reserves of 2000 as a basis for the calculation — this would mean that as of 2005 we would be down to a 12,842-day supply of oil.[35] That is just 35 years. On the other hand, production and consumption have been growing faster than the reserves, so that even this estimate could be optimistic.

Another factor that should be taken into account is the reduction of the useful life of the wells currently in production. What is happening in the North Sea will happen in the other oil-producing regions of the world.

---

32. Table 32
33. Table 31
34. Table 35
35. =Reserves/Production

WAKE-UP CALL

But the real problem is not how much longer oil will last. Even if it holds out for a few more decades, the world urgently needs to prepare for the transition to an unknowable future. And the effects of the first shock when people begin to realize what is happening are unimaginable. How will the last scarce barrels be allocated, and what will be the political, economic and military consequences?

Can a substitute for oil be found, in the medium or long term? The history of the world is the history of great changes, the history of transformations. As coal replaced wood and oil replaced coal as an energy source, tomorrow another fuel could replace oil. But when? How long would it take to adapt all our infrastructure to the new technology? And finally, the big question: where should we direct our research, the funds, the talent, the time: Natural gas? Solar energy ? Eolic energy? Biomass? Geothermal energy? Nuclear energy? Hydrogen? Something else?

CHAPTER 13. A LOOK TO THE PAST

FROM KEROSENE TO GASOLINE

Petroleum products found their way into our hearts and homes gradually. In the beginning they were used as fuel for illumination, and kerosene competed with candles, or with oils of animal origin and vegetable origin. Until the year 1911, kerosene was the main product of the petroleum industry. It was the invention of the combustion engine that generated the great petroleum revolution. When Henry Ford began production of the automobile, gasoline moved ahead of kerosene. This new mode of transportation, faster and able to go longer distances, transformed life. It is in the transportation sector that oil still has the greatest use, but today almost the entire industrial structure of the world depends on oil.

The world has never yet experienced a crisis from lack of oil. The price shocks of 1973 and 1979 were caused by political decisions, as the Arab countries moved in reprisal for the help the Western world gave to Israel. But a genuine crisis of supply, per se, has not yet been seen. But when that moment comes, oil will cease to be a resource of the oil countries, for the oil countries to manage. As long as oil has been abundant, the oil producers have retained a degree of sovereignty; but when the oil shortage is apparent, the gloves will come off and the competition between the various world powers will create a new political and military situation.

We Are Already at War

Seen retrospectively, oil exercised a fundamental influence in the two world wars, as much in their origin as in their outcomes. The naval superiority that gave the victory to Great Britain in the First War was owed, in good measure, to the decision of the First Lord of the Admiralty, in 1911, Winston Churchill, to use oil in place of coal for the English Army. It took only a few hours to equip one ship with oil and only a few men were required to execute that work; to supply ships with coal required hundreds of men and far more time. Britain's main antagonistic, Germany, maintained its coal-fueled fleet, a circumstance that hindered its capacity to maneuver. In the Second World War, oil was of paramount importance. With the industrialization of automobile and truck production, troop movements no longer depended on horse (or foot) power and the whole logistical concept changed. With motorized forces, armies could advance over great distances and could combat simultaneously on several fronts.

The development of aviation and its progressive incorporation into the military forces opened another important market for oil. Airships were fueled with an oil derivative. The consumption of aviation fuel in Great Britain quintupled between the beginning and the end of the war.

Germany paid very dearly for its lack of oil. Germany was defeated when its divisions were caught between winter and the Soviet offensive. What if they had had enough fuel to move their forces quickly?

Aware of this weakness, the Germans looked for ways to take advantage of the resource that they did have, coal, and they succeeded to produce synthetic fuel. They also managed to build a vehicle that required only a small amount of combustible fuel and did not use water; the Volkswagen was a commercial success for many decades after. But the production of fuel from coal was very expensive and production volumes were restricted; this fuel could not compete with oil. Germany used synthetic fuel from coal during the whole Second World War, but it never had sufficient quantities to satisfy its needs. One of Hitler's objectives in Russia was to take possession of the oil reserves in the Caucasus region, and perhaps from there to invade the Middle East. But the oil supply failed and he stopped at Stalingrad.

Japan's involvement in the Second World War was directly tied to oil. Japan was dependent on the United States for oil, which placed it in a highly vulnerable position. When the US threatened to cut supplies, Japan had to take radical action.

In 1999, it was announced that oil had been discovered in Vietnam. The reserves had always been there, and the technology to detect them was available in the 1960s. This raises the question whether the possibility of obtaining oil in Vietnam influenced the United States in its decision to go to war.

In spite of, or in addition to, all other possible factors that contributed to the first Gulf War and now the Iraq War, the urge to take control of some of the greatest oil reserves in the world, and the desire to put more Western military installations in the region, should not be underestimated. How many other conflicts have had similar objectives?

At least for a few years after the first Gulf War, oil was pumped and prices were kept stable. This situation continued until March 1999, when OPEC sought to reduce production and raise prices. From then on, oil prices have maintained an upward trend.

This illustration of the law of supply and demand was for some reason ignored by the managers of the Venezuela petroleum company between 1994 and 1998. They boosted production and argued that this would lead to a price drop in the first stage but that afterward, once demand had increased to meet those high volumes, prices would automatically go up. This was a thesis that flew in the face of everything economists had established as to the workings of the market. The objective of the managers was to saturate the market. As a consequence, Venezuelan reserves were quickly drawn down and prices dipped to the lowest levels since 1973, $7 per barrel. But when OPEC cut output in 1999 to begin a process of price recovery, the price rose above the $30 per barrel mark in just a few months. The old days of price stability are gone, and although one might see how the prices are changed, it is not always clear whose interests are being served one way or the other.

The Performance of Non-OPEC Countries

Norway and Mexico acceded to the decisions of OPEC in 1999 and oil prices started to go up. Norway was aware that its wells in the North Sea were losing ground. With the purpose of prolonging their production for a while longer, Norway has said it is willing to close two of its three platforms in the North Sea. Likewise, Mexico has had to invest in costly new technologies to recover the pressure in its oil fields in regions like Cantarel. According to external audit reports, the oil reserves of Mexico fell from 44 to 28 million barrels in 1999. Facing the reality of depleted reserves, the non-OPEC countries have the same interest as the OPEC countries to conserve the reserves they have and to receive a higher price for what they produce.

THE PRODUCERS

More than 60% of the world's oil reserves are in the Middle East. In 1860, when the commercial exploitation of oil began, in the United States was the largest producer and exporter in the world. By 1955, North America had become a net importer.

Starting from the Arab embargo of 1973, political and economic relationships shifted. For the first time oil was used as a political weapon. The Arab countries wanted to force the United States to press Israel to return the territories conquered during the Yom Kippur War to the Palestinian population. The Arab countries achieved none of those political objectives. But the embargo had a great impact in the industrial nations and the rest of the non oil-producer countries. Poor countries were forced to take on enormous debts to meet their fuel needs. Even rich countries felt the pinch, through higher prices and the simple fact that gas pumps were running dry. The consumer countries reacted and adopted measures to reduce their consumption and dependency on oil, with relative success. They began the search for alternative sources of energy and took measures to use oil more efficiently and to create strategic reserves for critical situations.

The 1973 oil crisis had several antecedents. In the early 1950s, King Farouk of Egypt was overthrown and a nationalist official, Gammal Abdel Nasser, assumed power. He sought to become a leader of the Arab world and he proposed using oil as a political weapon. Egypt was not an oil country; however, Nasser convinced some of the leaders of Arab oil countries that they had common interests, and in this way he began to influence politics in the oil world. The main objective of Nasser and of the other Arab leaders was to support the Palestinian population and to weaken Israel. In October of 1956, Nasser attempted the first oil embargo against the West and Israel. An important element in the plan was the closing of the Suez Canal, forcing oil tankers to detour all the way around Africa. The Canal was closed for eight years, between 1956 and 1964.

The West responded by seeking new oil supply sources in African countries like Libya and Algeria. By the middle of the 1950s, Libya — a country governed by a regime friendly to the West — turned out to have great potential and it was soon being exploited. But through a coup, Muammar Kaddafi assumed power. He threatened to nationalize the assets of the foreign oil companies operating in Libya if they did not agree to his terms; oil prices and the taxes on oil companies went up. The example of Kaddafi was followed by the rest of the oil countries. The Organization of Oil Exporters Countries, OPEC, was created in 1960 but this organization did not have any influence on world politics until 1973.

CHAPTER 14. PRODUCTION AND PRICES

HISTORICAL OVERVIEW OF PRODUCTION AND PRICES

Now we will review oil production and prices for the 140 years from its discovery in 1859 to 2000. The history of how this substance became vital worldwide is outlined in *Oil Facts and Figures* in its centennial edition of 1959 and of 1971.[36]

The most salient fact in the history of oil is the constant growth of production, with very few exceptional moments. The only significant downturn in the 19th century was in 1876, when production diminished by 16.1%. Production fell only 5% in 1930 as an effect of the Great Depression. A recovery began as soon as 1933. In 1942, production declined by 5.7% and in 1949 it declined by 0.8%. From then on, the growth trend was sustained until 1975, when it fell by 5.5% as a consequence of the embargo of 1973. In 1981 the biggest drop in the 20th century was seen: 6.4%. From then until 2000, production occasionally experienced a slight slow down but nothing significant, as shown in the figures.

Prices in the first two decades of production between 1860 and 1880 averaged around $3 per barrel. In the forty years between 1880 and 1920, the price stayed at about $1 per barrel. From 1920 to 1950, it fluctuated between $1 and $2.51 per barrel; this maximum was only reached in the last three years of the 1940s. From 1950 to 1972, the price was under $2 per barrel. Since 1973, oil prices began to climb, reaching a price of $32.5 in 1981, with spikes above $40.

---

36. Oil prices used in this section from 1860 to 1958 correspond to the average US price. After 1960 they correspond to the price of Arabian light crude.

THE 1860: GAS LAMPS AND GASOLINE

On August 27, 1859, Edwin L. Drake drilled the first commercial oil well in the town of Tusville, Pennsylvania. The next May, production began in West Virginia, Kentucky, Ohio and Tennessee. Also in 1860, the first Oil Workers Association was created and Edwin L. Drake was elected president. The average production for 1860 was 1,300 barrels/day; in just five years, production was up to 7,400 barrels/day.

By 1865 the first machines for the production of gasoline and gas lamps were built. On July 15, 1867, the first experimental use of oil as a locomotive fuel took place at the Warren and Franklin Railroad of Pennsylvania.

Table 129. World. Crude Oil: Production and Prices. 1860s.

Years	Production	% Change	Prices * *
	*thousands of barrels/day**		*$ barrel*
1860	1,3		9.60
1861	5,8	346.2	0.52
1862	8,4	44.8	1.05
1863	7,4	-11.9	3.15
1864	6,3	-14.9	8.15
1865	7,4	17.5	6.59
1866	10,6	43.2	3.75
1867	10,1	-4.7	2.40
1868	10,9	7.9	3.62
1869	12,8	17.4	5.60
1870	15,8	23.4	3.90
	Average Growth of Production		Average Price
	46.9		4.39

Sources: * Oil Facts and Figures. 1971 Edition. American Petroleum Institute. P. 556 and 557
* * Idem. Centennial Edition 1959. Pages 40 and 41.

THE 1870S: THE FIRST INTERNAL COMBUSTION ENGINE

Oil production was increased ten times in the 1870s, and it reached 15,800 barrels/day. Asphalt came into vogue for paving city streets (first tested in Newark, New Jersey). In 1872 the first gas pipeline was installed to bring natural gas to the population of Tusville, PA.

In 1875, the year Alexander Graham Bell invented the telephone, oil production reached 36,000 barrels/day.

In 1879, George Selden requested the first patent for an automobile equipped with an internal combustion motor. Thomas Alva Edison invented the incandescent lamp. Oil prices reached a maximum of $4.4 in 1871 but ended the decade at about $0.94 per barrel.

Table 130. World. Crude Oil: Production and Prices. 1870s.

Years	Production	% Change	Prices * *
	*thousands of barrels/day**		*$ barrel*
1870	15,8		3.90
1871	15,6	-1.3	4.40
1872	18,8	20.5	3.75
1873	29,6	57.4	1.80
1874	32,6	10.1	1.15
1875	36,0	10.4	0.97
1876	30,2	-16.1	2.52
1877	43,1	42.7	2.38
1878	50,4	16.9	1.17
1879	64,6	28.2	0.86
1880	82,2	27.2	0.94
	Average Growth of Production		Average Price
	19.6		2.17

Sources: * *Oil Facts and Figures. 1971 Edition. American Petroleum Institute. P. 556 and 557*
* * *Idem. Centennial Edition 1959. Pages 40 and 41.*

THE 1880S: THE FIRST GASOLINE STATION

Another unprecedented jump brought oil production to 82,200 barrels/day in 1880, more than doubling in five years. On May 24, 1883, the Brooklyn Bridge was inaugurated. In 1885, the first gas pump was invented. Oil production was relatively stable, at 100,700 barrels/day. Oil was the preferred fuel for lighting at this time. In this decade, the price was steady at less than $1 per barrel.

Table 131. Total World. Crude Oil Production and Prices in the 1880s.

Years	Production	% Change	Prices * *
	*thousands of barrels/day**		*$ barrel*
1880	82.2		0.94
1881	87.6	6.6	0.92
1882	98.2	12.1	0.78
1883	82.8	-15.7	1.10
1884	98.5	19.0	0.85
1885	100.7	2.2	0.88
1886	129.4	28.5	0.71
1887	130.9	1.2	0.67
1888	142.9	9.2	0.65
1889	168.5	17.9	0.77
1890	209.9	24.6	0.77
	Average Growth of Production		Average Price
	10.5		0.82

*Sources: * Oil Facts and Figures. 1971 Edition. American Petroleum Institute. P. 556 and 557*
* * Idem. Centennial Edition 1959. Pages 40 and 41.

THE 1890S: THE FIRST DIESEL MOTOR

But in 1890 production doubled to 209,900 barrels/day. In 1893, the first great shipment of refined petroleum products took place through a 252-mile pipeline in Pennsylvania. By 1895, production was 284,000 barrels/day. Were competitors in the offing? In 1896, H.A. Becquerel discovered the radioactivity of uranium and in 1898 the Curies discovered radium. In the same year, the first diesel motor was built in the United States.

Table 132. Total World. Crude Oil Production and Prices. 1890s.

Years	Production	% Change	Prices * *
	*thousands of barrels/day**		*$ barrel*
1890	209.9		0.77
1891	222.1	14.8	0.56
1892	243.1	9.5	0.51
1893	253.1	4.1	0.60
1894	244.7	-3.3	0.72
1895	284.0	16.1	1.09
1896	312.8	10.1	0.96
1897	334.2	6.8	0.68
1898	342.4	2.5	0.80
1899	359.3	4.9	1.13
1900	408.5	13.7	1.19
	Average Growth of Production		Average Price
	7.9		0.82

Sources: * Oil Facts and Figures. 1971 Edition. American Petroleum Institute. P. 556 and 557
* * Idem. Centennial Edition 1959. Pages 40 and 41.

THE 1900S: THE FIRST AUTOMOBILE AND THE FIRST FLIGHTS

In November of 1900, the first Automobile Fair was held in New York. Oil production reached 408,500 barrels/day.

In the 19th century the United States was the world's greatest oil producer. However, production was also beginning in Europe, Russia, China and in some distant areas of the American Far West.

In December of 1901, Marconi sent the first transAtlantic radio message. Two years later, in June of 1903, two events occurred that would directly impact the oil industry. Henry Ford created the Ford Motor Company; and the Wright brothers joined the club of aviation pioneers, Brazilians, Romanians, Frenchmen and others, with their initial flight at Kitty Hawk.

Oil production grew to 589,200 barrels/day. Oil prices were stable.

Table 133. Total World. Crude Oil Production and Prices. 1900s.

Years	Production	% Change	Prices * *
	*thousands of barrels/day**		*$ barrel*
1900	408.5		1.19
1901	458.7	12.3	0.96
1902	498.1	8.6	0.80
1903	533.9	7.2	0.94
1904	597.1	11.8	0.86
1905	589.2	-1.3	0.62
1906	584.2	-0.8	0.73
1907	723.1	23.8	0.72
1908	781.6	8.1	0.72
1909	818.3	4.7	0.70
1910	897.9	9.7	0.61
	Average Growth of Production		Average Price
	8.4		0.80

Sources: * *Oil Facts and Figures. 1971 Edition. American Petroleum Institute. P. 556 and 557*
* * *Idem. Centennial Edition 1959. Pages 40 -41.*

THE 1910S: WORLD WAR I

In 1910 production was at 897,900 barrels/day. Aviation was developing and oil derivatives began to take on greater importance. The first transcontinental flight, from New York to Pasadena, CA, took place In September 1911. Two years later the Panama Channel was completed. The first phone line linked New York to San Francisco in 1914. Oil price was still less than $1 per barrel.

Table 134. Total World. Crude Oil Production and Prices. 1910s.

Years	Production	% Change	Prices **
	*thousands of barrels/day**		*$ barrel*
1910	897.9		0.61
1911	943.4	5.1	0.61
1912	965.5	2.3	0.74
1913	1,055.7	9.3	0.95
1914	1,116.5	5.8	0.81
1915	1,183.6	6.0	0.64
1916	1,253.4	5.9	1.10
1917	1,377.7	9.9	1.56
1918	1,379.4	0.1	1.98
1919	1,522.9	10.4	2.01
1920	1,887.3	23.9	3.07
	Average Growth of Production		Average Price
	7.9		1.28

Sources: * Oil Facts and Figures. 1971 Edition. American Petroleum Institute, p. 556 and 557.
** Idem. Centennial Edition 1959. Pages 40 and 41.

In 1915, production was at 1.18 million barrels/day. In 1918 the first gasoline pipeline began operation in Wyoming, covering a distance of 40 miles. And 1919 saw the first oil-fed burner used to produce central heating in homes.

In 1920, production reached 1.88 million barrels/day. Of course, the First World War (1914-1918) had much to do with that. In this decade oil prices began to move, and reached $3.07 in 1920, the highest figure in forty years.

THE 1920S: REBUILDING AFTER THE WAR, AND THE GREAT DEPRESSION

Between 1920 and 1925, immediately following the First World War, oil production increased from 1.18 million barrels/day to 2.9 million barrels/day.

Table 135. Total World. Crude Oil Production and Prices. 1920s.

Years	Production	% Change	Prices * *
	*thousands of barrels/day**		*$ barrel*
1920	1,187.3		3.07
1921	2,098.6	76.8	1.73
1922	2,553.1	21.7	1.61
1923	2,788.8	9.2	1.34
1924	2,778.9	-0.4	1.43
1925	2,925.8	5.3	1.68
1926	3,004.9	2.7	1.88
1927	3,459.1	15.1	1.30
1928	3,629.5	4.9	1.17
1929	4,070.8	12.2	1.27
1930	3,868.2	-5.0	1.19
	Average Growth of Production		Average Price
	14.3		1.61

Sources: * Oil Facts and Figures. 1971 Edition. American Petroleum Institute. P. 556 and 557
* * Idem. Centennial Edition 1959. Pages 40 and 41.

In 1930 oil production rose to 3.8 million barrels/day. This means that it tripled, even though it was exactly in this period that the Great Depression took place. Oil production only dipped by 5% between 1929 and 1930. The first electric diesel railroad was brought into service in New York in 1925, and in 1927 Charles Lindbergh flew from New York to Paris. And in August of 1930, construction was completed for the first multiple pipeline to transport various petroleum products, extending from Texas to Illinois and then to Indiana.

The late Thirties was a period of reconstruction after the Great Depression; oil production rose to 5.8 million barrels/day in 1940. The Spanish Civil War (1936-1939) was a conflict in which all the world powers were involved, although this was not openly declared. Germany and Italy openly supported General Francisco Franco's Falange forces and the Soviet Union supported the Republicans. In the 1930s oil prices reached $1.18.

Table 136. Total World. Crude Oil Production and Prices. 1930s.

Years	Production	% Change	Prices * *
	*thousands of barrels/day**		*$ barrel*
1930	3,868.2		1.19
1931	3,763.4	-2.7	0.65
1932	3,589.8	-4.6	0.87
1933	3,947.9	10.0	0.67
1934	4,168.4	5.6	1.00
1935	4,534.1	8.8	0.97
1936	4,908.3	8.3	1.09
1937	5,586.5	13.8	1.18
1938	5,446.6	-2.5	1.13
1939	5,715.5	4.9	1.02
1940	5,889.9	3.1	1.02
	Average Growth of Production		Average Price
	4.5		0.98

Sources: * *Oil Facts and Figures. 1971 Edition. American Petroleum Institute. P. 556 and 557*
* * *Idem. Centennial Edition 1959. Pages 40 -41.*

THE 1940S: THE SECOND WORLD WAR

Between 1940 and 1945, oil production grew from 5.8 million barrels/day to 7.1 million barrels/day. The US government rationed gasoline from July 1942 until the war ended in August 1945. New pipelines were inaugurated to convey refinery products, including the Little Big Inch that extended from Texas to New Jersey.

D-Day, June 6, 1944, when the Allies invaded Normandy, required a secure fuel supply for the invasion forces; Operation Pluto, by which fuel was brought across the English Channel, has been called the greatest effort in the history of fuel transportation.

On August 6, 1945, the atomic bomb was dropped on the city of Hiroshima.

When the war was over and reconstruction through the Marshall Plan began, production grew to 10.4 million barrels/day.

In Indochina another local intense conflict began. At end of the 19th century, Vietnam was in hands of France. But during the Second World War Japan invaded it; in 1945, the allies defeated and expelled the Japanese forces and Vietnam was declared an independent country. But North Vietnam, supported by communist China, attacked the south and the French forces that were still there. So began a war that would culminate ten years later, in 1954, by means of a treaty that divided the new Republic of Vietnam in two, separated by the 17th parallel.

On average, oil production grew by 6.1% during the 1940s. The prices also went up, to $2.60.

Table 137. Total World. Crude Oil Production and Prices. 1940s.

Years	Production	% Change	Prices * *
	*thousands of barrels/day**		*$ barrel*
1940	5,889.9		1.02
1941	6,083.9	3.3	1.14
1942	5,734.5	-5.7	1.19
1943	6,182.5	7.8	1.20
1944	7,102.1	14.9	1.21
1945	7,108.7	0.1	1.22
1946	7,521.7	5.8	1.41
1947	8,279.8	10.1	1.93
1948	9,406.1	13.6	2.60
1949	9,326.3	-0.8	2.54
1950	10,419.2	11.7	2.51
	Average Growth of Production		Average Price
	6.1		1.63

Sources: * *Oil Facts and Figures. 1971 Edition. American Petroleum Institute. P. 556 and 557.*
* * *Idem. Centennial Edition 1959. Pages 40 and 41.*

THE 1950A: THE SUEZ CANAL CRISIS

In the first five years of the 1950s, oil production increased by 48%. Transcontinental television was inaugurated in September of 1951 and the construction and launching of the first atomic submarine, the Nautilus, took place on January 21, 1954 in Connecticut. Meanwhile, Korea was still occupied by the Soviet Union in the north and the United States in the south, and in 1948, the communists proclaimed a popular republic in the north. In June 1950, North Korea attacked South Korea, beginning the war that would last up to 1953.

Table 138. Total World. Crude Oil Production and Prices. 1950s.

Years	Production	% Change	Prices * *
	*thousands of barrels/day**		*$ barrel*
1950	10,419.2		1.71
1951	11,733.5	12.6	1.71
1952	12,414.0	5.8	1.71
1953	13,145.3	5.9	1.93
1954	13,744.7	4.6	1.93
1955	15,413.3	12.1	1.93
1956	16,778.5	8.9	1.93
1957	17,645.1	5.2	1.90
1958	18,128.6	2.7	1.85
1959	19,543.1	7.8	1.70
1960	21,026.0	7.6	1.55
	Average Growth of Production		Average Price
	7.3		1.80

Sources: * Oil Facts and Figures. 1971 Edition. American Petroleum Institute. P. 556 and 557.
* * Idem OPEC. Price nominal. Price official of the Crude Arabian Light.

In the last five year of the 1950s, oil production was up 36%. At this time, Egypt took control of the Suez Canal. This fenced in Israel, cutting off supplies. It also disrupted commerce for many Western countries.

Even so, world oil production grew by 7.3% during the 1950s, and the price remained stable.

THE 1960S: THE SIX DAYS WAR

In the early 1960s, production increased by approximately 50%. In May 1967, Israel invaded and took control of the Sinai Peninsula in the Six Days War.

The conflict in Southeast Asia continued to escalate.

Oil production rose to 35,291,000 barrels/day, and kept rising; in this decade it averaged 8% growth.

Table 139. Total World. Crude Oil Production and Prices. 1960s.

Years	Production	% Change	Prices * *
	*thousands of barrels/day**		*$ barrel*
1960	20,934.0		1.55
1961	22,343.0	6.7	1.45
1962	24,263.0	8.6	1.40
1963	25,960.0	7.0	1.40
1964	28,071.0	8.1	1.35
1965	30,201.0	7.6	1.35
1966	32,812.0	8.6	1.35
1967	35,291.0	7.6	1.35
1968	38,054.0	7.8	1.30
1969	41,246.0	8.4	1.25
1970	45,272.0	9.8	1.67
	Average Growth of Production		Average Price
	8.0		1.40

Sources: OPEC Annual Statistical Bulletin 1989. Page 12, 15.
* * Idem OPEC. Price nominal. Price official of the Crude Arabian Light.

THE 1970S: THE ARAB OIL EMBARGO

With the Suez Canal closed and Westerners feeling a little more pliant, in January 1970 the new President of Libya, Muammar Kadafi, forced the oil companies to pay a higher price for Libyan crude. Libya became a leading oil producer and its strategic location on the Mediterranean Sea facilitated oil transport to Europe. This was the first time that an OPEC country used its influence to increase the price of oil.

In 1973, the Yom Kippur War took place, in which the Arab countries reclaimed the territories that Israel had taken during the Six Day War. On the brink of defeat, Israel requested and obtained help from the US, which turned the tables in favor of Israel. This led the Arab countries to declare an oil embargo against the Western world. And the embargo was a big success. The Arab nations reduced their production of oil and adopted a series of measures to keep their oil from transiting through third countries to the United States and other allies of Israel. Oil prices jumped like never before. In 1974 it hit $10.70.

Table 140. Total World. Crude Oil Production and Prices. 1970s.

Years	Production	% Change	Prices * *
	*thousands of barrels/day**		*$ barrel*
1970	45,272.0		1.7
1971	47,854.0	5.7	2.0
1972	50,708.0	6.0	2.3
1973	55,478.0	9.4	3.1
1974	55,813.0	0.6	10.7
1975	52,746.0	-5.5	10.7
1976	57,566.0	9.1	11.5
1977	59,806.0	3.9	12.4
1978	60,265.0	0.8	12.7
1979	62,800.0	4.2	17.3
1980	59,767.0	-4.8	28.6
	Average Growth of Production		Average Price
	2.9		10.27

*Sources: * OPEC Annual Statistical Bulletin 1981; 1982; 1990.*
* * Idem OPEC 1998. Price nominal. Price official of the Crude Arabian Light.

THE 1980S: THE IRAN–IRAQ WAR

From November 1979 to November 1980, oil reached a new high, $40 (in 1980 dollars) and it stayed above $20 until 1986. The early 1980s saw a crisis created by the overthrown of the Shah of Iran and the setting up of a theocratic government opposed to the Western world. In 1981, oil production suffered its biggest drop in history, 6.4%. This and the drop recorded during the 1929 Great Depression are unique historical moments.

Table 141. Total World. Crude Oil Production and Prices. 1980s.

Years	Production	% Change	Prices **
	*thousands of barrels/day**		*$ barrel*
1980	59,826.0		28.6
1981	56,027.0	-6.4	32.5
1982	53,739.0	-4.1	32.4
1983	52,803.0	-1.7	29.0
1984	53,118.0	0.6	28.2
1985	53,291.0	0.3	27.0
1986	56,289.0	5.6	13.5
1987	55,377.0	-1.6	17.7
1988	57,863.0	4.5	14.2
1989	58,637.0	1.3	17.3
1990	60,384.0	3.0	22.3
	Average Growth of Production		Average Price
	0.2		23.90

Source: OPEC Annual Statistical Bulletin 1982; 1984; 1985; 1989; 1999.
*** Idem OPEC 1998. Price nominal. Price official of the Crude Arabian Light.*

THE 1990S: THE PERSIAN GULF WAR

THE 1990S: THE PERSIAN GULF WAR

In 1990, as a first consequence of Iraq's invasion of Kuwait, the price was $20 but began to come down and by December 1998 the OPEC price of reference was $9.69. Then OPEC began a price recovery campaign, and the world was paying $30 dollars by 2001. Then came the destruction of the World Trade Center in New York, when prices fell significantly — albeit temporarily.

Table 142. Total World. Crude Oil Production and Prices. 1990s.

Years	Production	% Change	Prices * *
	*thousands of barrels/day**		*$ barrel*
1990	60,384.0		22.26
1991	59,069.0	-2.2	18.62
1992	59,752.0	1.2	18.44
1993	59,312.0	-0.7	16.33
1994	59,945.7	1.1	15.53
1995	60,325.8	0.6	16.86
1996	61,433.7	1.8	20.29
1997	62,853.7	2.3	18.68
1998	65,013.9	3.4	12.28
1999	63,368.1	-2.5	19.31
2000	65,824.9	3.9	30.37
	Average Growth of Production		Average Price
	0.9		19.00

Sources: * *OPEC Annual Statistical Bulletin 1990; 1995; 1999; 2000*
* * *Idem OPEC 1998. Price nominal. Price referential of the basket OPEC Spot.*

Prices had been heading upward since 1999; in August 2005, they hit a new apex at more than $60.[37] One might predict that this is only a taste of what is to come.

---

37. BP Statistical Review of World Energy June 2005.

Figure 26.

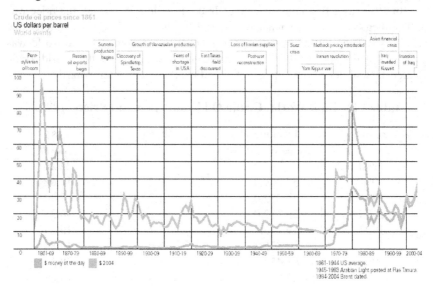

Source: BP Statistical Review of World Energy June 2005

CHAPTER 15. WHAT NEXT?

THE NEW CHALLENGE TO THE ECONOMY

In terms of economic theory, the main point of this book is that we need to take a new view of the factors of production, a change of 180 degrees from the traditional concept. Since its birth as a modern science, economics has considered that the scarce factor of production is capital. The statistics presented above show that this is about to change. Natural resources, first and foremost potable water and conventional oil, are in very scarce supply and this must now be considered the most important economic fact.

This means changing the whole paradigm of the economy. From the economic point of view, global production of goods and services will be affected in quality as much as in quantity; that, in turn, will affect prices and inflation levels. And from the human point of view, a real global scarcity of natural resources will vastly affect the quality of life in the developed nations and the odds of survival in the undeveloped nations.

Consider that the glaciers of the Himalaya are melting; those glaciers nurture six of the main rivers of Asia, the Ganges, Indus, Brahmaputra, Thanlwin, Mekong, Yangtze and the Yellow River. In the US, where the Colorado River feeds the Southwest, cities and farmers have long been fighting over water rights. In Latin America, Brazil for one had to impose water restrictions in 2002; in Africa and the Middle East, the most emblematic rivers like the Nile, the Jordan, the Tigris and the Euphrates already present serious problems. The Sahara Desert is expanding and more and more territory has become uninhabitable. And the statistics on conventional petroleum reserves show that conventional petroleum is on the verge of being used up.

That is the real scenario; and all of the aspects of the problem as enumerated above are only a few signs of that reality. Interpreted properly, the signs can show us what may happen in the future.

GENERAL CONCLUSION

The world is facing an unprecedented problem. As the population continues growing, demand for oil and other resources goes up while pollution and climate change reduce the available quantities. Urgent, concerted action is required. But do we have the political will to make tough choices?

Constant economic growth and globalization cannot go on in an unlimited way forever, because the earth's resources are not unlimited. More efficient technologies and alternatives can go a long way to extending the time frame, but the end must be the same. Sooner or later, things run out. Technology cannot replace Mother Nature as a primary source; it can only improve the yields.

The great challenge to science is to find ways to use fossil fuels more efficiently while reducing their harm to the environment, and to produce substitutes in an economically and ecologically viable form. The great challenge to political and cultural leaders is to address the shortages with some honesty, to help people understand the need for restraint, and to maintain some degree of peace and stability in the coming difficult times.

No one can expect the population of the Third World to relinquish their claims to a share of the resources. But all of humanity may be requested to use the resources more rationally. If under normal conditions the oil producing countries are the focus of the attention of the word's leading nations, under extraordinary conditions the producing countries would lose all semblance of sovereignty as the strongest nations expropriate the oil. And then, all bets are off.

It is necessary also to point out that only a conservation world program that has one of their fundamental objectives to diminish the levels of contamination in all the orders, to eradicate nuclear tests, to revert the damages caused to the forests by reforesting the areas already depredated –the reforestation to a world scale would be a palliative in front of the great damage caused by the greenhouse effect — and the development of highly efficient technologies polluting the least possible, only could we assure the continuation of the life in the future. For a very simple reason: because the production and consumption pattern followed up to now by humanity — and the one that will be derived of the economic growth of the undeveloped countries — it is simply unattainable to a medium term.

If more oil is found, if technological advances make alternative energy sources economically and practically viable, if we can reduce the pollution and at least slow down the destruction of the environment, then we will have a reprieve, perhaps gaining enough time to make a turn around. But so far, this ship is still moving fast and in the wrong direction. There is no sign of a miracle on the horizon.